TWO AND TWO
MAKE FOUR

TWO AND TWO MAKE FOUR

BY

BIRD S. COLER

NEW YORK
FRANK D. BEATTYS AND COMPANY
1914

THE DE VINNE PRESS

CONTENTS

PREFACE

TWO AND TWO MAKE FOUR

How did man learn that two and two make four? Did he discover it, or was he told? It is an interesting question. Some very celebrated scientific students would insist upon a scheme of life which identifies this knowledge that two and two make four with a certain agitation of the constituent atoms of the brain. These scientific students are for the most part dead, now, it may be worthy of note, and the celebrated scientists of the present day, for the most part, have a different idea of the case.

But plain men can very well leave this question to warring scientific schools. We know that two and two make four. We have a constitutional difficulty in assenting to any statement which depends upon the supposition that two and two make five. In our business a five-dollar obligation will not be satisfied with a two-and-two settlement. This book is the application of this very primitive logical principle to history and science. It is the use, in the examination of historical statements and scientific teachings, of the common sense that God has given us.

When we want a house built we hire a good builder, but we do not accept the house, if it is a bad house, just because the builder was a good builder. Neither should we accept a historian's conclusions simply on the ground that he is reputed to be a good historian, nor a scientist's conclusions simply on the ground that he is a good scientist. "Your researches may have been extensive," we may say to both of them, "but this matter of two and two is not a matter to be upset. We do not know about those things you have found under the microscope, Mr. Scientist, or those things written on ancient parchments, Mr. Historian, but we know that two and two make four."

The reader who follows me through these pages will find some questions that are in the realm of history, some that are in the realm of sociology, some that are in the realm of philosophy. He will find them just as I found them in my study of the causes of an obvious and unpleasant fact. The public schools in this country are not making for righteousness. There isn't an educator of any note in this country who hasn't admitted this. The metropolis of this country is thug-ridden. It has developed a new type of criminal, a conscienceless, fearless young brute who murders for hire, and recognizes no moral accountability and no social obligation. "Gunmen" and murder-procurers have had their activities exposed in court. There is a similar state of affairs in Paris. Probably it is a little worse there. This is "two." In Paris and in New York there are godless public schools. In

PREFACE

Paris atheism is a little more bold, a little more positive, than in New York. This is also "two."

The relationship of the godless school to the growing viciousness among our people did not come to me as a religious man. As a practical man, a public officer administering a municipal office, I was called upon by my official duties to pass upon the expenditures of public money for charitable purposes. I found, as a matter of cold fact, that the mortality rate in state institutions for the care of the weak and helpless was terribly high, while in similar institutions under the care of religious bodies it was quite low. This interested me, and an inquiry resulted, which revealed the truth that in the care of the helpless those who have the service of God at heart are more efficient than those who are mere servants of the state. If this were true of foundling-asylums, why not of schools? Quite by accident the obvious relationship between the godlessness of the public school and the poor moral and mental character of its products forced itself on my attention. The next step was to look for the cause of the godlessness of the public school, and by the two-and-two method I found this quite clearly in view. It was a prejudice which came from two directions. Following it to its source, I found it ultimately political in both directions, although from one it appeared in the disguise of a religious and from the other in the disguise of a philosophical prejudice. The prejudice from the second direction was assuming a larger importance because of the pseudo-philosophy back of the political movement that embraced and developed it. A study of this philosophy by the two-and-two method discovered the vice at the heart of it. Its operations in France furnished concrete examples. There it had boldly attacked all religion. There and here it had common characteristics; there and here it sneered at morality, bitterly assailed religion, and sought to gain converts by divorcing religion from education. That this is not an accidental but an essential part of the movement is apparent. John Spargo, American Socialist writer, in his "Socialism," says:

"Whether the Socialist régime could tolerate the existence of elementary schools other than its own. such as privately conducted kindergartens and schools, religious schools, and so on, is questionable. Probably not. It would probably not content itself with refusing to permit religious doctrines or ideas to be taught in its schools, but would go further, and, as the natural protector of the child, guard its independence of thought in later life as far as possible by forbidding religious teaching of any kind in schools for children up to a certain age. Beyond that age, religious education, in all other than the public schools, would be freely permitted. This restriction of religious education to the years of judgment and discretion implies no hostility to religion on the part of the state, but neutrality. Not the least important of the rights of the child is the right to be protected from influences which bias the mind and destroy the possibilities of independent judgment in later life, or make it attainable only as a result of bitter, needless, tragic expression."

The result is an increase in illiteracy in France, and a deterioration in the quality of education here, considering the matter from a secular standpoint; and a riot of murder and lawlessness in Paris and New York, considering the moral aspect. In France and here an emphasis upon eugenics is characteristic of the movement. The beloved Darwinian theory of "natural selection" is to be abandoned for a theory of artificial selection. The result in France is an alarming fall in the birth-rate. Here it has not had time to work out yet, but there are signs. The two-and-two method would indicate a remarkable resemblance in results between eugenics and what Colonel Roosevelt calls "race suicide." I have heard of the marvellous subtlety of the Jesuits, but they could, if they were all their enemies conceive them to be, or accuse them of being or having been, evolve no more efficacious scheme for getting rid of Protestantism than the preaching of eugenics among non-Catholics. A century and a half of eugenics would leave the Catholics in possession of the earth.

PREFACE

And this brings me to the other aspect of this prejudice. Its study, by the two-and-two method, has brought me face to face with a great church and the facts of its history. They were of intense interest to me because they were new to me. From conventional history I had acquired the conventional Protestant view of this church and its relations to civilization. The two-and-two method gave me a new view-point. I found that this church had been a defender of civilization in the past, and was the defender of civilization to-day. That was not conventional history, but it was the truth, and as the truth I set it down.

I have said that a century and a half of eugenics would leave the Catholic Church alone in the field. A century and a half of the godless school would leave the same church in complete possession of Christianity; and such a school as Spargo says will be compulsory under Socialism would put that church to the necessity, under which the early fathers labored, of resorting again to the catacombs in order to protect the faith from a hostile world. I have little respect for the strength of faith of those members of my own creed who fear the triumph of another church as a result of religious teaching in the schools; and I have less respect for their judgment, for it is plain to me that Catholicism can stand up against a state-supported educational system from which God is excluded, and equally plain that Protestantism cannot, and that the

PREFACE

result of the public policy so many Protestants now
blindly support will be a complete extinction of their
branch of Christianity and a division of the world of
opinion between Catholicism on the one hand and
atheism on the other.

TWO AND TWO
MAKE FOUR

TWO AND TWO
MAKE FOUR

CHAPTER I

CHURCH AND STATE

IF you stand before a steam-boiler you will see a
small glass tube containing some water. The
water in the tube rises and falls. This is a gauge
—the proportion of the water in the tube to the capacity of the tube is always the proportion of the
water in the boiler to the capacity of the boiler. You
cannot see the water in the boiler, but this is an un-
failing index, this gauge; never higher will the water
rise, visible, in the tube of glass, than it rises, invisible,
in the boiler.

What the glass tube is to the boiler, such is the
thing we call the government to the mass of our people. It is one of the gauges of our national morality,
one of the many indices by which we may know what
is the average of morals in our people. There are
other indices—commercial life is one. Never will government rise higher morally, nor will business morality make a higher mark, than the average morality
that we cannot see, nor otherwise measure, in this
huge mass of ninety million human beings. The law
of balance is perfect—it is what we call the law of

averages, the law of compensating forces, the law of the conservation of energy, the law of gravity, the law of harmonics. We have many names for it—one, which is comprehensive, is the Eternal Justice of God. That is at the heart of it; that is why all these laws that we meet in physics, in music, in chemistry, in astronomy, in anything whatsoever, are in reality the same law. Truth is true universally.

It is my idea, then—and not mine alone but that of many—that a good citizen must be first a good man. I do not mean a perfect man, any more than I mean a perfect citizen; human nature being what it is, we can hope for neither. But I do mean a man with an impulse in the right direction and the grace to be ashamed of what things wrong he may do: with a developed conscience.

I cannot conceive of a bad man being a good citizen. By a bad man I mean, not a man who sins, even though his sins be grave, but a man whose impulse is toward sinning, whose conscience lies atrophied and tongueless in his breast, who cannot be said to have fallen before temptation because he never has stood up before temptation.

It has been the experience of the human race that mere intellectual culture does not vivify a conscience. It must be inspired—*breathed into*. And only God can breathe life into it, as God only can breathe life into anything that lives. Behind morals, therefore, there must be inspiration. Behind the good man there must be the idea of God.

It has been the expressed opinion of the most, and the best, educators, and students of education, that this thought of God should be instilled into the consciousness of youth; that religious education should be mingled with secular education, the one to animate and make beneficial the other. So many are the students of life who have declared non-religious education a thing dangerous to the state that I shall not name them here; enough of them for the purpose I shall name elsewhere.

In this country we have laws making education compulsory because we believe, and the fathers of the Republic believed, that it is good for the state that all its rulers should be intelligent. The compulsion lies not only on the child to receive, but the parent to furnish, and not only the parent but all adults; it being the theory that an educated people is a state benefit shared in by all the citizens. The state makes itself the agent of the citizens in this matter, taking from them a part of their income, as John Stuart Mill points out, and, with the fund thus obtained, building school-houses and hiring professional teachers.

The system, as it exists at present, is by no means what was planned at the outset. The planning was vague and meagre, sufficient unto the day and place; what we now have is something that has been shaped and fashioned by developments of the intervening years which were not thought of in the beginning. One idea with regard to it, which had to do with other things as well, found a place in our fundamental law, and by a strange misconception, not of its purpose but of its operation, it has come to operate inversely. The idea was that public funds should not be used by one creed, or religious denomination, to the prejudice of any other; that there should be no discrimination against any religion. Upon the perfectly sound theory that a discrimination in favor of any religion would be a discrimination against all other religions, we have done a most unsound thing; that is, we have laid down an iron bar of discrimination against all religion. The engine that we built to go has gone, but instead of going forward it has gone backward. Our state, that was not to discriminate against any man's belief in God, has crushed out of its school system all belief in God.

Our effort to be just was until recent years universally honest, and is still for the most part honest; and this outcome is quite unexpected and perplexing. Men at the head of our educational institutions who have no desire for anything like this, who feel the evil of it, for some years now have been puzzling their brains in an effort to think some way out. They have advanced many ideas: first, agreement of Protestant sects upon form of religion to be taught; then agreement of Protestant and Catholic divisions of Christianity; still later, agreement of Jewish and Christian leaders. That has been going on for some years, but instead of getting better the thing gets worse. We are so many denominations; naturally, there can be no agreement. Every step we take leads away from the ideal, every change is one in the direction of an absolute divorce of religion from education. How is this to work out? Some men are trying to substitute for the old religious inspiration something that will check the spread of immorality. It is to be ethical training—they are going to teach ethics. But Dr.

Andrew S. Draper, State Commissioner of Education in New York, remarks dubiously, "If it is difficult to separate religion from morals, it is *dangerous* to separate ethics from morals." Dr. Draper is struggling with this problem from his own standpoint—What are we going to do to make our present public-school system efficacious morally? In his *Religion, Morals, Ethics, and the School,* published by the New York State Education Department in 1911, he speaks of the situation in France, where they have gone the full length of the formula. Read what he has to say and make what you can of it. Is it good? Is it bad? It is hard to tell just what Dr. Draper's conclusion is on the whole question. But it cannot be wholly good, for he finds some "trouble" about it. "Political and religious freedom have been enlarging their opportunities under the French Republic," Dr. Draper says. "In doing so they have been seeking education that is not limited by the dogmatic teaching of a church. And thus they have been pulling down a church without reforming it or putting another in its place. It is to be feared that this has been destroying faith altogether. Instruction about the moral virtues without faith and feeling may result in the superficial politeness which is perhaps a little better than savagery, more than in the sound character that is infinitely better than either."

This is Dr. Draper's opinion with regard to it. There are others who say baldly that it has resulted in the savagery itself; we shall hear them later.

But what concerns us now is that our machinery isn't working right; it isn't doing the thing we builded it to do. And it won't ever do it; it will always get worse and worse; and the more swiftly because there is a new force at work which this machinery, working backward, suits in every rod and wheel. What we intended as a device for insuring religious liberty, Socialism finds admirably adapted to its work of crushing religion out of existence altogether, in order that its political power shall grow out of its materialistic philosophy. Under the skilful operation of its Intellectuals our public-school system is producing a generation of atheists.

Now comes the question, Are we wedded to the machine or the ideal? Are we going to give each church, as each man, equal opportunity to grow and function, or are we going to make religion and individual life mere state functions?

Some of our churches, seeing the trend of all this, have taken steps of their own. The Roman Catholic Church cannot longer see its children attending a godless public school, and it has built up its immense system of parochial schools. The Lutheran Church is doing the same thing in the Middle West; the Hebrew congregations are doing it more or less extensively; other churches are doing it, here and there. All these schools, furnishing secular education of as good a quality, and often of better quality than the state furnishes, are supported by private contributions. The communicants of these churches have voluntarily assumed a burden rather than risk the souls of their little ones. All are taxed for the public schools, and they are thus compelled to pay for a system of education which they believe to be bad for the children who receive it and bad for the state that furnishes it, as well as the cost of the schools they themselves maintain. The believer in God and democracy is saying to himself, "This American Republic, which I love and would preserve, is taking a part of my income to build up a huge campaign fund for a Politico-Philosophical Party that hates it and would destroy it. Is it right?"

It isn't right. It is in every aspect altogether wrong. And what is more, the way to stop it is simple and obviously just. It is proposed to make the education of each child, by whomsoever, the unit basis for the expenditure of funds raised for school purposes. It is proposed that if a church furnish education sufficient to enable a child to pass a state examination, then the state shall pay that church for the work done, whether that church be Protestant or Catholic or Hebrew. It is proposed to pay any non-religious organization in the same way and upon the same basis.

In these payments nothing whatever is to be allowed for sectarian or proselytizing instruction. It is merely, in the cases of churches, the hiring of God-believing forces to do secular work. It is allowing the plain people to send their children to authoritative moral schools if they so desire, by the state devoting that part of their wages to the secular support of such schools which they themselves would naturally employ for that purpose were not their revenue reduced by state school taxation. It is allowing the parents to bring up their children in the faith of their fathers without compelling them to submit to double school

[9]

taxation as a penalty for so doing. It is allowing the parents to direct the use, under proper supervision, of that portion of their earnings which is taken from them by the state for educational purposes. It is compulsory state education under the direction of the parent as to that part of it which is moral. It is not the forcing upon the children, against the will of the parents, of state socialistic theories by teachers of faiths other than their own, or of no faith at all.

This is the simple plan proposed for rounding out the education of the youth of this country; for checking the spread of materialism and its dominance in our public-school system. It is the only plan possible, it seems to me, in a state whose mighty population is divided into many creeds. It is unjust to no denomination; it would give light and latitude for the growth of all denominations.

Why, then, if this plan be simple and just, and its object on all hands admittedly desirable—nay, more than that, necessary to the continuing righteousness and strength of the state—why is it not put in operation? Why do not those who admit that there must be some moral element in education, who admit that it is not there now, and seek in many places for some method of putting it there—why do not they give their support to this plan, demanding of legislatures that it be enacted into statutes, telling of it to the people until the people unanimously write it into the fundamental laws that are made at first hand and are called constitutions? What stands in its way?

A fear. A fear that was born of a prejudice. A fear that is strong because it is not a fear of the ignorant

and the thoughtless, but one that holds in its grip
men of culture, men who have read widely and
thought deeply. It prevails among these, not because
they have failed to look at the facts of history, but
because they have accepted a false theory as to the
meaning of those facts. It is not ignorance, it is a
wrong point of view. And the point of view was the
prejudice out of which this fear was born.

It is easier to name this fear than it is to define it;
easier to tell how it is called than what it is. It is
called "Church and State." If I ask one man, "What
is 'Church and State'?", he will answer, "The Spanish
Inquisition," and it may strike me that it is called, not
the Church Inquisition, but the *Spanish* Inquisition.
If I ask another he will answer, "St. Bartholomew,"
and I wonder if the Guises were the Church or the
State. I shall get many answers: "Temporal Sovereignty," "The Holy Roman Empire," "The Concor-
dat," "The excommunication of Philip Augustus": all
ancient and modern instances of supposed Roman
Catholic ecclesiastical interference with temporal government.

None answers me with a reference to the union of
Church and State under Henry VIII of England, or
the German Electors, or under the Czars of Russia. It
is quite plain that we do not think of these instances
when we talk of "Church and State"; what we do
think of is a Roman Catholic alliance with the governing power. What we think to-day is precisely what
was thought in England three hundred and many
years ago, when it was reported that the Jesuits were
welcome guests in the palaces of the Stuarts. The

viewpoint has come down to us unchanged, and it never occurs to us to challenge it, to question whether it was right or wrong, to consider whether even, if it was right then, it may not be utterly wrong now; for there have been changes—the state does not now mean what it meant when Louis XIV truly expressed the thought of monarchs in his "L'Etat, c'est moi!"

What does the state mean—here and now? It means you and me. It means the government of the people by the people. It means something that cannot become subservient to any creed until there is among the people a substantially unanimous adherence to that creed.

Even if the church desired it. And does the church desire it? Has the church ever desired it? It was to the political advantage of rulers and parties some centuries ago to give to the people the viewpoint that the church did desire it. It was to their political interest to picture a church constantly intriguing, constantly reaching out for temporal power; and writers of popular history were influenced—in most cases, I believe, honestly and unconsciously—by the national or party viewpoint, and read into history a meaning that it did not have of itself. Historians of the present day are beginning to recognize the error of that viewpoint, the fallacy of the earlier inferences, and to clear up some of the confusing conceptions that have so long clouded the vision of the English-speaking world. Without extenuating the cruelty of St. Bartholomew's bloody massacre, they have recognized it as the punishment by a prince of seditious subjects, a movement that was base and bloody *and political*.

Without palliating the cruelty of the Spanish Inquisition, they have recognized it in its cruellest aspect as a national rather than a church institution; something that belonged to the Spanish character, and, following upon the freeing of Spain from the yoke of the infidel, was inspired more by personal and political vengeance than by attachment to the church. It was as easy for a politician in those days, using religion as a mask, to have an opponent's head cut off, as for a political boss in later days to use his leadership to deprive an enemy of his livelihood.

They are recognizing the political significance of the status of the papacy prior to the Reformation; they are understanding that the interdict laid upon Philip of France was the punishment of an individual for a moral wrong, and could have had no effect whatsoever were it not for the assent of the French monarch's subjects to its justice.

We do not have to wait upon the historians, however, for a reasonable view of the meaning of history. If we are furnished with the facts, we can form our own conclusions; we may be startled to find them, when formed, far away from those we have been accustomed to accept as they have been handed down to us. The facts, or enough of them to serve as a foundation for proper conclusions, are easily obtained. We need not seek for them in manuscripts that are obscure as to meaning and difficult of access; we can accept those which have been familiar to students of popular history for generations. And, if we wipe away all religious prejudices, all preconceptions of what kind soever, and simply let our conclusions grow from the facts before us, we shall find those conclusions within striking distance of the truth. The change of viewpoint will give us a new vision. The whole picture changes as the facts of history rearrange themselves, falling into their proper places and perspective, and we are astonished to find how well balanced, how symmetrical the whole is.

CHAPTER II

WHAT THINGS ARE OF CÆSAR

IT would be impossible in such a work as this to treat the relationship of church and state exhaustively, to follow the thread through the tangled skein from the beginning up to the present hour. And it is not necessary. If we test a stream at various points and find the water sweet at every point tested, we can very safely assume that all the stream is sweet. If, therefore, wherever we touch the history of the church we find an insistence upon a certain policy, we may as safely assume that that policy was fundamental in the church institution, in accord with the spirit of the Redeemer when he talked to the apostles. That insistence we do find, running through entire ecclesiastical history. It breaks out at the very beginning in the answer of Christ to the Pharisees: there are things that belong to Cæsar and things that belong to God. There is a distinction between the church and the state. The state has to do with the comfort and convenience of man in this world; the church has to do with his eternal salvation. The state concerns itself with man in his social organization, the church with his individual soul. The law of the state rests justly upon the welfare of the community; the laws of the church upon the mandates of the Creator.

This was a novel idea in the Roman world when

first Christianity attracted the attention of men. In all the pagan world religion had been a function of the state. The gods of Rome were *officially* the gods of Rome. Their priests were government officials, the Roman emperor was pontifex maximus of the Roman religion. It had always been so in the world the Romans knew. Deities were national; the Greeks had their gods, and the Carthaginians. It was the political aspect that first made Christianity odious in the eyes of the Roman rulers. The offense of the Christians was that they were obstinately disobedient to the laws and disrespectful to the gods of Rome. Their sin was sedition. That was why they were hated, that was why they were persecuted.

In the days of the early Christians, and for generations before that, there was no spirit of religious bigotry among the Romans. The masters of the world were broad in their worship; they admitted the gods of all nations to their temples. But they were intensely patriotic. They were devoted to the Roman laws. And the offense of the Christians was not that they worshiped a strange God, but that they refused to bend before the Roman law. As yet the people of Rome could not understand the distinction between church and state; they were all one in the Roman mind.

It took centuries to get the new idea into the mind of the public. Indeed, there is doubt as to whether the work has yet been done. But the idea has been always in the church. It taught it to the Romans themselves, to the slave and the freeman, the beggar in the market-place, the tradesman in the bazaar, the smith in his forge, the soldier in the field. That was why, toward the end of the pagan dispensation, Roman generals found Christians among the bravest and most faithful of their officers and legionaries. The soldiers of Rome were attracted by the high courage of the Christians; in the spirit of men and maidens who could die smiling for a faith there was something akin to their own dauntless spirit.

Indeed, long before Constantine the Christian faith had won its place in the world. Constantine plucked the ripened fruit. That was the reason the Roman world became Christian in his day; that was the reason that within a single generation a proscribed and treasonable faith became the faith of the Roman government.

The fruit had been ripening for more than three centuries. The pagan gods had become too numerous to be respectable. The human heart knew the difference between good things and bad things: a proof more conclusive than many of the premises of so-called scientific philosophy that *good and evil are facts*. Under the gay worship of Saturn and Bacchus, and the libidinous devotion to Venus, there was among the pagan peoples a strong moral sense that made it difficult to adore such divinities. Greek and Roman had felt this: the Greek because his intellectual nature demanded virtue and justice in a god as a matter of logic; and the Roman because he was at heart a sober, continent being. In other words, before the revelation came to either, the mind of the Greek and the heart of the Roman knew what a God was like. They had pieced together, after a fashion, the necessary attributes of divinity until they had the outline of the Portrait.

They had got beyond the stage at which philosophy hails worldly happiness as the sum of good. In the upward march their philosophy had accepted the necessity of suffering and sacrifice; had grasped the truth that indulgence cannot be ennobling. Our Rationalists, and particularly our Socialistic Rationalists, are going in the other direction; their trend is toward that barbarism from which the old philosophy was then emerging to meet the Truth.

In the East humanity groped with speculative hands for something solid in a fluid universe; something fixed in a world of motion; something stable in a world of change; something that would endure while all else was disintegrating. The mind of the Roman, less given to speculative exercises, still sought something which would make men strong in body and in soul. The message of the Christian apostles met the need of both; it fulfilled the Greek's speculative yearning; it gave the food for soul and body that the Roman demanded. And it gave more than either demanded. For the first time these peoples felt the glow of a religion that was on fire. For the first time a living force that was not of the earth touched them and stiffened their moral muscles for the work that was to be done. They were lifted up and driven forward; high courage emboldened their hearts and a divine effulgence lighted their minds. First in the hidden places underneath the ground, then in private houses, and at last in their own temples, they gathered in increasing numbers to worship Jesus Christ.

With a little thought and a little knowledge we can get the spirit of that time and understand the sentiment of the pagan world with regard to the new faith. It was known that it had been born in Judea, and the first impression was that it was Jewish in its entirety. Then there was some confusion because the recognized leaders of the Jewish world became the most bitter of its foes and the most cruel of its persecutors. It found its first converts—Gentile converts—where the need of justice is always the greatest: among the poor and the lowly. The essential democracy of it made it strong among the common people; it was an inspiring thought for the despised laborer and the down-trodden slave that in the eye of God he was the equal of emperor or master. We are all the children of God, of whom he loveth one not more than another.

Among the great and influential it was still regarded as not only a foreign, but a vulgar, superstition. The philosophers of the time, the men whose comments give us the light we have on the thought and manners of their day, were amazed, as was Pliny, at the obstinacy of the new teachers in their refusal to obey the Roman law with regard to the worship of the Roman gods.

But little by little the Roman world was being won, trusted slaves were telling their virtuous masters the story of Bethlehem and Calvary, scholars were beginning to read the letters of Paul, soldiers were hearing around the camp-fire of the devotion and the courage of the new sectaries. By channels multifarious and devious the new faith was working its way in the

Roman body politic. The rude hostility of the mob, and the philosophic contempt of the wealthy and the educated, were gradually being overcome. Men great in the sanctity of their lives had been leaders of the church from the first, but soon they became great also in other respects—great in courage, great in mental as well as moral strength. No longer the Christians worshiped underground. They began to build churches on the surface, and the churches were crowded. Their organization followed the Roman eagles over the world; there was the church in Rome, the church in Asia, the church in Alexandria. Their priests preached the gospel of Christ to the veteran warriors who held the Caledonian wall in far-off Britain, as well as to those who faced the Parthians in the East and those others who watched the Germanic barbarians in the long marches beyond the Rhine. Great orators spoke from the Christian pulpits and marched boldly into the courts of the Cæsars to plead the church's cause to the emperors themselves. The cry of the mob was no longer, "To the lions!" "God and the Mother of God!" became a well-known street cry in Rome and the Roman dependencies. Persecutions were periodical, not constant; in the periods of non-molestation the church developed its organization and builded its great temples. Half the population of Alexandria filled the streets in protest against the persecution of their bishop.

It has long been a matter of controversy as to whether the conversion of Constantine was a real conversion, or merely the far-sighted move of a consummate politician. We Protestants have been wont to upbraid our Catholic brethren for the honor in which they have held the name of Constantine. It has been charged that his glorification by the church was due very largely to the material benefits he conferred upon the bishops. Quite enthusiastically we have gone about the work of showing him to be not a great saint, but a great sinner. In the meantime we have quite overlooked the fact that a considerable number of us Protestants, who are not Mormons either, have overlooked the peccadilloes of Henry VIII, because of his services to the Protestant cause. What matters it now, save perhaps to Constantine himself, whether he was a great saint or a great sinner? He was probably both; the sins and the virtues of his time were extreme.

The truth, in all likelihood, is that Constantine was influenced by both political and religious motives in accepting the new faith. His inclination from childhood had been in that direction. Constantius, his father, was a friend of the Christians, and the favorite officers of that beloved general professed the new faith. When he died and the British legions elevated his son and invested him with the purple at York, many of the sober, disciplined veterans who raised him aloft and saluted him as Cæsar were worshipers of Christ. Looking across the wide reach of Roman dominion, he could see dangers ahead, and the mind of so shrewd a student of men, so able a politician, could hardly overlook the advantage of an alliance with a church whose organization threaded every part of the Roman world, whose followers were among the bravest and the best in every Roman legion. Side by side with this was his temperamental inclination. His was a great mind, and it revelled in the glory of the Christian faith. His intellect and his heart were attracted, his interest was engaged; all things worked together to make him a Christian.

But there had been bred in the bone the old Roman tradition that the state was supreme; that the church was its servant. The new conception maintained itself in his mind with difficulty; his lips gave support to it, but time and again the impulse to control the organization of the church, to bend it to compliance with his own will, manifested itself; and this was responsible for the beginning of that long contest between church and state which has never ceased. This was the occasion for the first conspicuous assertion by the church of the doctrine that there are things that are of Cæsar and things that are of God; that between the functions of the state and those of the church there is a real distinction.

It is not difficult to understand the mental attitude of the first of the Christian emperors. His father had been a soldier of the old Roman type, strong in mind and body and austere in habit and thought. The Greeks were marble, the Romans granite, men. Constantius had all the Roman's lofty and stern contempt for the softer things of life; the indulgences of the stay-at-homes had no charm for the stalwart soldier of the empire, whose business it was to keep unbroken the outer line of the Roman domain. The traditions of old Rome were dear to him, and the ideals to which he held himself he set up for his son. For him the old gods were respectable because they were the national gods; for him religion was part of the business of the state. Indeed, the state he served was his whole life; a glory greater than the national glory he could not understand, a power greater than the civic power was not conceivable.

Constantine grew up under his father's eye and under his father's tutelage. He inherited the traditional conception of the supremacy of the state. It was bred into his being, and it outcropped many times in those later days when he had become the sole and supreme ruler of the Roman world and the imperial patron of the Christian church. In his repeated expressions that he was a priest of the church, that he was its soldier and its guard, we can see the effort he was making to bring his mind into consonance with the doctrine of the church; but in his attempt to govern the bishops, in his letters upon matters of doctrine to the warring African ecclesiastics, is observable the old tradition, the hereditary temper, against which the church made its early protest. Again and again it was pointed out to the imperial convert that in matters of policy and organization his advice and assistance were welcome and his commands enforceable; but that in matters of doctrine he *must* abide by the law as revealed.

Constantine's conversion was proclaimed on his march from Gaul to Rome in the year 312. He was then one of the three Cæsars who governed the Roman world. But a year before the last of the great persecutions had been officially closed by an edict issued in his name and that of his senior colleagues, Galerius and Licinius. In fact, it had closed before

that; there had not been for some years any attack
upon the Christians by the government, but nevertheless the Roman law was affirmatively a hostile law,
and the Christians lived in peace only because it was a
sleeping statute within twelve months of the public
announcement of the young emperor's conversion. It
is strange to read the name of Galerius at the foot of
the edict of toleration that killed the sleeping statute,
for it was Galerius who inspired the persecution of
Diocletian, and it was the same rude graduate of the
camp who sullenly yielded to the logic of the changing hour and was forced to acknowledge that the obstinate adherents of the new faith could not be
brought back to the gods of old Rome: but, on the
other hand, had so far extended their influence that
continued persecution had no other significance than
the proscription of perhaps a majority of the Roman
people. Tormented by disease, perplexed by the ever-
increasing might of the religion he could neither
understand nor destroy, the beaten Roman bowed his
obstinate head to what he had come to recognize as
the inevitable, and in substance said what Julian was
to say later, "The Galilean has conquered." For the
strong arm that had been Rome's boast, the sword
that had been a staff that never failed her, were un-
availing against Christianity, and Galerius knew of
no other weapon.

Following upon the first edict of toleration came a
second, signed at Milan by the Christian Constantine
and the pagan Licinius, and the accelerated transition
from the old order to the new is illustrated in the
warmer tone of the Milan decree. No longer is it a

precarious privilege which the Christians are to enjoy, but a free and unconditional right.

There was more than the edict itself might indicate. A Christian emperor was now well on the road to supreme power in the state, and his zeal for the religion he professed influenced in growing degree the policy of the government.

The immediate effect upon the church organization was profound. Hitherto the ecclesiastical office had been one of labor and of danger. The bishop occupied a perilous eminence; his breast was the target of the arrows of the enemies of the church. Upon his head the state visited its punishment of the church. The rewards of his office were not measured in the wealth of the world. Now, there was a precipitous change: no longer was there danger from the agencies of the state, but, on the other hand, the whole power of the state was exercised in the protection of the bishop. No longer was he without influence in the civil tribunals: his words were potent in the ears of the mighty ones of earth. No longer was he the persecuted priest, but a powerful prelate in whose anterooms waited a constantly increasing crowd of clients, as the greed and the ambition of the Roman world turned to face the rising sun. The lustre of the pagan temples was dimmed, the secular glory of the Christian church grew constantly more effulgent.

Inevitably came the evils inseparable from such a condition. The flood of worldly honor and material wealth swept from their feet some of the churchmen, and the episcopal office became vastly important from a political standpoint. If the church were the road to the affections of a prince whose favor was so productive of earthly riches, then be sure that those who sought the riches of earth took the road that led thereto.

Not always, then, did the bishops draw clearly the line between what Constantine might legitimately do and what he might not do. These old priests were human, they were grateful to the prince who had left the old national belief to bow his head before the true God, and some of them turned to him for advice on subjects which lay without his domain. But although some of them did this, not all of them did, and the church itself never conceded to him the right to pass upon questions of doctrine. It was always the schismatic who appealed from the synod to the emperor; the orthodox church held always to the unchanging truth of the doctrine deposited with it.

Constantine understood this attitude of the church, but his zeal to prevent strife among Christians upon points which seemed to him immaterial, coupled with the imperious temper, led him from time to time to overstep the boundary line between his legitimate sphere of influence and that of the church. "I am in a sense a bishop," he said once, "but a bishop of the external." Again, when the Donatist schismatics appealed to him from the decision of the Synod of Arles, he exclaimed: "They demand judgment of me—of me who await the judgment of Christ! But I say the judgment of priests ought to be regarded as if the Lord himself sat in the tribunal. What, then, do these wicked men, truly instruments of the devil, mean? They institute an appeal in this as in a purely civil case."

WHAT THINGS ARE OF CÆSAR

This Donatist controversy was one of the first political troubles that vexed the early church. Cæcilian had been elected bishop of Carthage, and his enemies, of whom he seems to have had quite a number, conspired to oust him from the place. Their zeal seems to have increased as the office became more important politically, and there was intervention on the part of outside forces who deposed the bishop and elected one Donatus in his place. Throughout the Christian world this proceeding was regarded as illegal; on the question of the legitimacy of Cæcilian and his innocence of the charges brought against him by the Donatists, the church authorities were all in concord. This was proven when the Gallic bishops concurred with the Roman pontiff in the Lateran Council, convoked at the request of the emperor, who explained in a letter to Pope Miltiades that his purpose was to prevent a schism in the church. Its ruling did not satisfy the Donatists, and in response to their importunities the emperor had a second synod convoked—the Synod of Arles. It assembled in 314 and made short work of the Donatist case. Once more the defeated party appealed from the ecclesiastical to the civil power, and it was this appeal that drew from Constantine the indignant exclamation quoted above. But the habit of command was strong in his blood; notwithstanding his Christian abhorrence of an appeal to the secular power in ecclesiastical matters, he *did* give a hearing to the pertinacious Donatists—a hearing which resulted in a civic confirmation of the ecclesiastical decrees condemning the enemies of the Carthaginian bishop. Although his decision was with the orthodox, it is none the less true that he assumed against the doctrine of the church the right of review.

If, in the first instance, the imperial power backed up the orthodox church, however, it did not do so in the second instance; that is, ultimately Constantine was opposed to the church, although he may have been—and indeed the evidence is that he was—unconscious of that opposition.

Arius, a priest of Alexandria, began during the second decade of the fourth century to preach a doctrine upon which was based the first considerable division in the Christian church. It was in effect that Christ was not coördinate with God the Father, but was merely the first-born of his creatures. This was declared by the church a denial of the divinity of its Founder, and Alexander, the bishop of Alexandria, took steps at once to silence the heretical expounder. The eloquence of Arius, however, and the eagerness of the public for novelty in an age of great and rapid vicissitudes of belief, gave to the preacher of the new doctrine a popular following not inconsiderable, and he refused to retract at the command of his bishop. Two bishops, Secundus of Ptolemais and Theonas of Marmarica, took up cudgels for the disobedient priest and defended his cause in the synod of the bishops of Egypt and Libya, convoked by Alexander to consider the case. This synod, held in Alexandria about 321, condemned the doctrines of Arius and excommunicated him and the two bishops who espoused his cause.

Complaining that he was suffering from the persecution of his bishop, Arius fled to the eastern provinces. Here he sought the protection of the favorites of Licinius, the rival and the colleague of Constantine. Among the converts he made was Eusebius, bishop of Nicodemia and powerful in the court of the Eastern emperor. The influence of Eusebius gave Arius a welcome among the Eastern bishops, and he soon numbered many of them among his supporters. Already there had broken out that disagreement between Constantine and Licinius which was to progress so swiftly to a civil war; and as the eastern and western sections of the empire took up arms for the political contest, so did the Roman world divide on the question raised by the preaching of Arius. The bishops of the East held a synod in Bithynia, and sent forth a request to "all the bishops" to hold communion with the Arians. Armed with the letter of his friends of the East, Arius returned to Alexandria, but the bishop of the African metropolis refused to receive him into the communion of the church.

Meanwhile the war had broken out and terminated, and Constantine, victorious over Licinius, and now supreme ruler of the whole Roman world, learned of the division in the Alexandrian church. His preoccupation in military affairs had prevented him either from knowing or from understanding the point in dispute, and, annoyed that the politically unified empire should be ecclesiastically divided, he addressed a letter to Alexander and to Arius, urging them to conciliation since the cause of their quarrel was not of importance, as he understood the matter.

But here was a question more serious by far than the Donatist matter. The former controversy had been mainly of church organization; this was doctrinal. Alexander refused to accede to the imperial wish; there could be no communion with an Arian in the orthodox church. One can imagine the surprise of the emperor when word of this was brought to him. It was one thing to advance the theory that the church was free in matters of faith; it was quite another thing for any subject to reject the plea of his ruler. The Christian patron of the church and the Roman ruler were brought face to face suddenly, like the images in and before a mirror. But it was the Christian theorist who was in the looking-glass; it was the Roman ruler who stood in flesh and blood and thought and felt. And it was in the breast of the Roman emperor that there was born a very human and altogether unchristian dislike of the Alexandrian church, which was to have its consequences later.

The alert mind of Constantine doubtless ran over the measures possible under the circumstances. He could use violence, the old weapon of the state, against Alexander, but this might mean warfare with the church he had so recently joined and a reversal of the whole policy which had elevated him to the greatest of worldly eminences. He decided against that. He must, even if his motives were wholly worldly and selfish (and in strict justice to him let us admit that they may have been—indeed, in all probability were— unselfish and religious), find a means of accomplishing his purpose without destroying the alliance between himself and the church, whose roots were shooting deeper and deeper into the hearts of men. He was surrounded by clerical counsellors, and their pleadings and his own desire to save the face in the looking-glass ran together; he convoked a general council of the bishops of Christendom to pass upon the Arian doctrines and other matters suggested largely by the ecclesiastics of the church in the East. For it was in the East that contentions arose in greatest measure; it was the bishops of the Eastern church who seemed to have yielded to the new influence introduced by the change in the relationship of the state toward the church; it was there that the courtier-prelates clustered thickest and the reverence for worldly power and the love of worldly emolument were most strongly mingled with the ancient spirit of the church.

It is significant of the rising influence of the Eastern as distinguished from the Western church in the court of the emperor that the first general council was held in Nice in Bithynia. The letter in which the ruler invited the bishops to assemble was full of expressions of esteem for them and their sacred office. In response to it there was an ecclesiastical migration toward Nice from all parts of the extensive Roman dominion. From the far provinces of the East and West, along the military roads and across the blue Mediterranean from the African provinces, came the shepherds of the flocks. Men who lived and prayed and preached in the remote parts of the empire, whose flocks were made up of the barbarians but recently conquered by the Roman legions, men whose fare was simple and whose purses were empty, found themselves provided with transportation, guarded by the soldiers of the empire, honored as princes by the state which only a few years ago sought them out for martyrdom with the keen edge of its sword. Simple of life and thought, they came hurrying toward Nice, eager to see this great emperor who had bowed the knee before the true God. May of 325 found them assembling in the city of Nice. The system of correspondence that had kept the church together had made even the most remotely placed members of the episcopate familiar with the names and actions of their colleagues, but we can fancy the wonder with which the bishops from the wilderness looked upon the splendidly garbed courtiers who shepherded the flocks near the heart of the empire. The emperor had not yet arrived, the strangers were received and entertained by the Oriental bishops; there were preliminary assemblages and private and public banquets; there was animated discussion of the great questions soon to come before the assembled council. The name of Constantine was on every tongue; what was he like? the strangers asked, and what he was like his familiars told them. Was it any wonder that the three hundred and eighteen bishops held their great assemblage back in order that they might elucidate Christian truth in the very presence of the mighty champion of the church? It was not that he had given them security and many of them wealth: he had given power and honor to the church, to the glorious faith to which most of them had proven their devotion by lives of privation and danger, and for which some of them had joyously endured the torture and seen their red blood flow.

When at last he came to Nice the council was solemnly opened. The bishops assembled, and Eusebius, himself an Eastern bishop and a church historian, tells us of the breathless silence in which they waited the coming of the emperor.

Constantine himself neglected nothing which might indicate his appreciation of the solemnity of the occasion and the feeling of honor he held for the church. He came, as that same ecclesiastical historian described it, "like a messenger of God, clothed in raiment which glittered as it were with rays of light; reflecting the flowing radiance of a purple robe, and adorned with the brilliant splendor of gold and precious stones." His speech no less than his appearance was likely to increase the favor in which the Christian priesthood already held him. It was full of devotion to the church, a division in which he regarded as more dangerous than any kind of war or conflict. To prevent such division he had called them together; ministers of God as they were and faithful servants of Christ, the Lord and Saviour, the spirit of peace and concord should prevail among them. He was their fellow-servant of God; he desired, above all things, that all cause of disunion among God's servants should be removed.

During the debates that followed the opening speech, Constantine carefully abstained from interference, except to counsel moderation in speech when some of the disputants became too fiery. Frequently an eager debater would turn with appeal to the splendid and mighty figure who sat among them, but the emperor let the current of opinion flow on without attempt to direct it. The conclusion he accepted without question. It was the codification of what was Christian truth according to those most competent to judge—the Nicene Creed. Three hundred of the bishops gave assent to that creed; five only dissented. Of these five three were of the Eastern church; two were the old friends of Arius—Theonas of Marmarica and Secundus of Ptolemais, who had defended him in the Alexandrian synod.

The council having determined the theological question, Constantine used the civil power to banish Arius and those who still adhered to his doctrine. He wrote to the Alexandrian church declaring that all should abandon the error of Arius.

The three Eastern bishops who had joined Theonas and Secundus in dissent from the Nicene Creed, could not, when the test came, bear to part with the offices they held. They were too much in the habit of bending before the secular power, and they reluctantly, and not very honestly, as future events were to show, subscribed to the conclusion of the majority of their colleagues. This reduced the number of dissenting bishops to two.

Constantine celebrated the close of the council with a great banquet, given to the bishops on the twentieth anniversary of his elevation to the throne. He exhorted the bishops from whom he was about to part to maintain peace in the church. Many believe it was at this banquet that he described himself as being in one sense a bishop: "You are bishops whose jurisdiction is within the church: I also am a bishop, ordained by God to overlook whatever is external to the church."

WHAT THINGS ARE OF CÆSAR

The Eastern bishops had been defeated in the council, but they by no means abandoned their hope of winning the mind of the emperor away from the orthodox church. They were not without powerful allies close to the imperial presence; Eusebius of Nicomedia possessed great influence over Constantia, the widow of Licinius and sister of Constantine. But a few months after the Council of Nice he and Theognis were charged with giving communion to the Arians, and that banishment they had escaped by subscribing to the creed was inflicted upon them.

Constantia exerted all the influence she possessed to bring about their recall and to incline the mind of the emperor toward the Arians. On her death-bed she requested Constantine to take into his service a priest who quickly won favor with him and who prevailed upon him to reopen the case of Arius. Eusebius and Theognis were recalled about this time, and by imperial edict their bishoprics were restored to them. Before the emperor, Arius made a profession of faith which Constantine accepted as in accordance with the Nicene Creed, and Eusebius immediately wrote to Athanasius, who had succeeded to the see of Alexandria upon the death of Alexander, urging him to restore Arius to the priesthood. But the profession of Arius was by no means satisfactory to the Alexandrian bishop, and he flatly refused to admit Arius to communion: refused not only when urged to do so by Eusebius, but also when commanded to do so by Constantine. And so for a second time the Christian votary and the Roman ruler faced each other. This time the situation was more serious; whereas Alexander had rejected his counsel, Athanasius had boldly disobeyed his command.

Under the influence of Eusebius, an influence which had been growing ever stronger in Constantine's court, orthodox bishops had been forcibly ousted by the emperor from sees in the East, and Arians had been appointed to succeed them. These new bishops united now to destroy the Alexandrian prelate. Charges were made against him which reached the emperor finally. It is notable that the charge upon which he acted was political altogether: Athanasius was accused of threatening to stop the shipments of corn from Alexandria. This meant the starvation of the capital, which drew its supplies of food from the Egyptian granaries, and the angry emperor banished Athanasius as a fomenter of discord in the church and an enemy of the state.

From that time on until the death of Constantine, an odd condition existed in the empire. Professing always his adherence to the Nicene Creed, Constantine yielded more and more to the influences that opposed it. He still maintained a friendship with the great lights of the orthodox church, but his policy toward the church was shaped and bent by the subtle bishop of Nicomedia, and by imperial edict priests who believed in the Arian doctrine were raised to the episcopate. The churchmen of the East became more and more fawners upon the imperial power; they planned to have Arius himself publicly and with splendid ceremony reinstated in the priestly office in the great church of Constantinople. Only the death of the arch-schismatic as the procession of his triumphant supporters marched to the church prevented them from carrying out this plan, and, by its effect upon the mind of the emperor at that time and in that place, checked for a while the Arian influence in the imperial court. It is said that as Constantine approached his end his dislike of Athanasius began to yield under the arguments of St. Anthony, but he died with the chief bulwark of the orthodox church still in that exile from which the second Constantine at last recalled him.

Briefly, then, this is the story of the relationship of Constantine to the Christian church. It was a tremendous period; its effect upon human history makes it stand out monumentally, but it is very far back on the road, and none too bright are the lights that glimmer fitfully upon it, illuminating it in spots. In such lights as we have, however, there are some things clearly discernible. We can see the influences of the old conceptions still at work, the old order endeavoring to maintain itself against the new. The nationality of religion was a habit of human thought, no less of the pagan Greek than of the monotheistic Hebrew.

"The independence enjoyed by these communities," says Ranke, "was not merely political: an independent religion also had been established by each; the ideas of God and of divine things had received a character strictly local; deities of the most diversified attributes divided the worship of the world, and the law by which their votaries were governed became inseparably united with that of the state." It was, to use the great German historian's own term, "an intimate union of church and state."

This conception carried itself into the Roman scheme of government as the conquering city, binding the conquered nations into her empire, gathered their gods together and gave them place in her Pantheon; it developed in its logical process until above the gods of all the nations it set the deified emperor, exalting above all the divinities the head of the Roman state.

It was this conception that Christianity had to fight. The battle was easier for the church when the state was hostile than when the state was friendly. Dimly, but unmistakably, the lines of the conflict disclose themselves in the Constantine period. We see the early divergence of the bishops of the East, who fawned at the feet of the emperor, from those of the West, who, with headquarters in abandoned Rome, had to work out the future of the church far from the seat of worldly power. The orthodox church was already insisting upon its spiritual freedom; the schismatics appealed from the ecclesiastical to the civil power. Well may we close this chapter with the words of Ranke: "The emperor united church and state: Christianity separated, before all things, that which is Cæsar's from that which belongs to God."

CHAPTER III

THE BIRTH OF THE PAPAL STATE

RACE prejudice is perhaps the strongest prejudice that human beings know. Its expression in mob action is merciless, murderous. It feeds avidly and grows enormously on calumny. It is permeated by an unshakable self-satisfaction that makes it opaque: the light cannot penetrate it.

Race prejudice is a parasite of patriotism; an evil growth on a good tree. The patriotism of the multitude becomes race prejudice in the mob. Ignorance fosters it; under that black shadow, love of one's own people is transmuted into passionate hatred of other peoples.

In the early middle ages the seat of ecclesiastical authority became a state. It is useless to deplore this fact. Superficial reviewers, who are friends of religion, regret it as the cause of corruption in the church organization and of division among the followers of Christ; superficial reviewers, who are enemies of religion, exploit it as irrefutable proof that the greed of men, and not any divine inspiration, was the soul of the ecclesiastical body. But the unbiased student will marvel at the strange combinations of circumstances from which there could be no other issue than the clothing of the Christian church with political power, and the student who holds the vast and sublime conception of the mission and destiny of the church can-

[39]

not escape conviction that the hand of God was moving among the nations. For, as one assembles the phantoms on the misty stage of the dark ages, and notes the political life that was generated in the dying body of the Roman Empire, as vermicular life in the human cadaver, the conclusion is irresistible that a measure of political power was absolutely necessary to the continued existence of the church. Under the idea of political supremacy, then and for centuries theretofore prevalent in the minds of men, it was impossible for the church to do its work while its central authority was in real political subjection to a secular sovereign.

While the Roman imperial organization, animated to the end, although in lessening degree, by the ancient democratic principle that government exists legitimately only for the welfare of all the people, held sway over the world, there was no serious friction, although the growing principle of autocracy had impelled rulers from the time of Constantine the Great to attempt the control and direction of ecclesiastical affairs. Had not the autocratic principle fastened itself upon the Roman political system, it is doubtful if there would ever have been any radical disagreement between the civil power and the church; for the church, by reason of its nature, could never have been in conflict with the democratic principle.

But when the corrupted heart of the Roman system could no longer send efficient impulses to its extremities, and the imperial power ceased to be a substance and became a shadow less and less distinct on the western world, it was necessary that some physical bulwark should be erected for the protection of the physical organization of the church, in order that the human depository of divine truth might continue to hold aloft for the illumination of the world the inextinguishable spiritual light.

There were sequential offshoots of this fact that were deplorable, beyond any doubt, but they were the evils necessarily concomitant with the imperfection of human nature; just as a tremendous effusion of blood was a necessary concomitant of the beneficent Revolution to which the world owes this Republic. And one of the collateral effects of the political status of the church was a factor making for race prejudice in the religious development of the world. The conflict between the Teuton and the Latin, the distrust of the stranger and the dislike of strange customs so natural in man, grew up between the children of the Roman civilization and the children of the forest barbarism which was conquered by and in turn conquered that civilization; and when there came a division on doctrinal points, racial prejudices so envenomed the controversy that it became the policy and the practice of Protestant princes to instil a horror of the ancient church and its leaders in the minds of their subjects.

To consider, calmly and without the prejudice that has so long clouded the Protestant mind on the subject, the beginnings of the temporal sovereignty of the popes shall be, therefore, the business of this brief chapter. It is the common understanding that this thing came about as a result of deliberation, as a consequence of the ambition and political ability of designing priests. A little reflection will show how far from the fact is this view of the subject; for the seed of the thing was in the ancient organization of the Church of Rome, a form of organization that existed for centuries before the church was recognized by the Roman state as anything but a criminal association of the obstinate votaries of an incomprehensible superstition.

The Church of Rome was democratic in the broadest sense. The bishop was elected by the communicants. When, finally, the whole population of the city of Rome became communicants, they became electors also, and they continued to act as such until mob violence made so great a scandal in the episcopal elections that it was necessary to place the power of selecting bishops in the hands of holy men; thereafter the clergy alone were to exercise the right of election.

But for many centuries the old system prevailed; for many centuries the Roman bishop was not only the apostolic successor of St. Peter, but the chosen man of the Roman people, their wisest and their saintliest man. Subject civilly to the emperor, he was yet a sovereign spiritual before whom the emperor bowed the knee. As the primate of Christendom, he enjoyed the respect and affection of even those barbarian peoples whose rising military strength was compressing the empire.

Keeping in mind this unique position occupied by the Roman bishop, let us consider the decline of the civil power to which he owed allegiance. At about the time that the proscription of the Christian church ended—and the coincidence is worthy of notice—the

Roman emperors abandoned the ancient capital. **Constantine** himself built his own capital, which **was to** serve for many hundred years as the seat of **the** Cæsars. The city by the Tiber became of secondary political importance; gradually it sank into the position of a duchy or military division of the empire. With his seat at Ravenna, an exarch, or vice-emperor, governed it in common with the other military divisions of Byzantine Italy.

The west and north of Europe had in the meantime been lost to the empire. In northern Italy the Lombard kings not only laughed at the Roman power, but more and more stretched their own boundaries over the Roman territory. Britain was a congeries of microscopic kingdoms; France and Germany were split up into principalities so numerous as to be confusing. The strong sword of an ambitious soldier carved out a state in a day, and the weak sword of his son lost it in an hour. There was no international law but the law of the strong hand. A man's kingdom was what he could hold in his grip; when his fingers weakened the kingdom vanished. Territorial lines flickered like the will-o'-the-wisp; to-day a town yielded allegiance to one king, to-morrow to another.

There was no such thing in Europe then as an army in the modern sense, or in the ancient Roman and Greek sense. A king was a leader to whom a number of feudal lords adhered, and his forces were the servants of his own household and those of his subject lords. The feudal system had supplanted the old Roman military system.

It is interesting to look back at the development of

the feudal system. It was the natural consequence of the system of delegated authority by which the Roman emperors, when they had lost the martial vigor of their predecessors, hoped to govern a vast domain without personal trouble. Certain districts were handed over to military leaders, or *dukes*, who were supposed to govern them in lieu of the emperor. These dukes parcelled out the districts among their officers, who were supposed to pay them a certain tribute and furnish them a certain number of men for military purposes. Each lord was a captain, each duke was a colonel, the emperor was of course the general; indeed, that is the meaning of the word *emperor*, just as *leader* is the meaning of the word *duke*.

The dukes were only temporary officers at first, during the period when the emperors personally knew the confines of the empire; but as it became too laborious for the luxury-loving successors of Constantine to travel any distance from their palaces and slaves, and not only the military roads fell into decay, but the Roman laws lost their binding force, making such travel difficult and dangerous, the Byzantine rulers troubled themselves little about the remote provinces, and each duke was left to his own devices and the choice of his own successor. His captains, very loosely bound to the remote imperial allegiance, were intimately connected with the more immediate incarnation of power and authority in their local leader.

Meanwhile the old democratic theory of government had been utterly lost. The imperial laws troubled but little these nominal officers of the empire, who now owed their real power to the soil rather than to the distant sovereign, and who knew the weakness of the living authority behind the written statute. Each leader was a law unto himself; sometimes he freely bound himself to allegiance to a leader stronger than himself, but it was an allegiance from which he relieved himself whenever his own strength and inclination moved him. Sometimes, when conditions made it convenient, a number of dukes would band together and elect a leader whom they would call a king; or, as was more often the case, a king would be elected by important families and lead them in war against neighboring dukes.

From out the northern forests came the Lombards, following the Goths, who had conquered and reigned at Ravenna and had then been displaced. They were at first less numerous, and therefore less powerful, than the Goths. Under Alboin, their king, they seized the northern part of Italy, and threatened but did not annex the lower provinces, which still owed allegiance to the Eastern emperor. Independent duchies, Beneventum and Spoleto, also arose and joined with the Lombard kings in threatening the dwindling Byzantine power. Luitprand, a later king of the Lombards, an enterprising and able chief, made extensive conquests, and his activity presaged a not distant subjugation of Ravenna and Rome. Classis, the seaport of Ravenna, was one of the cities that surrendered to his arms.

While the ancient capital was thus threatened with subjugation by barbarian forces, the interference of the Byzantine emperor in religious matters brought on a quarrel between the civil power and the church.

Leo the Iconoclast, backed by courtier-priests of the
Eastern church, questioned the spiritual superiority
of the Roman bishop, and the pope organized a resistance to the imperial mandates with regard to the use
of images. He was supported by the neighboring
duchies, whose people sent the representatives of the
emperor to Constantinople and selected as their own
leaders men who sided with the Roman Church. The
exarch Paul, under orders from Constantinople, sent
troops to Rome to enforce his master's decrees, but
the Lombard troops hurried to the defense of the
pope, and the troops of the exarch retired. In Ravenna Paul found the imperial troops in a mutinous
spirit, threatening to proclaim the deposition of Leo
and to elect an emperor in his place. The people of
Ravenna were so angered at the attack upon the pontiff that riots occurred, in one of which Paul was slain.
He was succeeded by Eutychius, who was the last of
the exarchs.

Eutychius at first thought to follow in the path of
Paul, but he soon found that he could not rely on his
troops in a warfare on the pope; he therefore made an
alliance with the Lombards, the object of which was
the complete subjection of the dukes of Beneventum
and Spoleto to Luitprand and the subjection of the
Roman pontiff to the Byzantine court. To Eutychius
it was soon apparent that the Lombard was much interested in the first part of the programme, but not
particular with regard to the second. After Luitprand had received the submission of the two independent dukes, he and they and the exarch went to
Rome to visit the pope.

There is a delightfully humorous flavor of modern politics in the history of that visit and its effects. Luitprand began diplomatically by overwhelming the pope with gifts. If the civil governor of the Romans, the duke, took part in the proceedings, as undoubtedly he did, his part is not considered of sufficient importance for historical record. It was the Roman bishop who entertained the visitors, and it was to the Roman bishop that Luitprand, who knew the real power from its counterfeit, paid homage. It did not take the kick of a mule, obviously, to indicate to Eutychius what the exact conditions were, and how little likely it was that his Catholic, if barbarian, ally was going to use any force in bending the pope to submission; for thereafter we find the exarch in quite amicable relationship with the pope, acting quite as the other dukes acted, and paying little attention to the distant emperor. All the comfort Leo might take from the fruits of Eutychius's expedition was an alliance of all three parties in Italy for the purpose of capturing a pretender to the Byzantine throne whose name was Tiberius.

But Luitprand soon found it convenient to war again upon the emperor, and Eutychius, as the representative of the emperor, suffered in consequence. The Lombard king made himself master even of Ravenna, and the exarch fled to Venice for refuge, and was reinstated in his duchy only through the intervention of Pope Gregory III.

All through his reign, which was long and prosperous, Luitprand was considerate of the rights and comfort of the pope and his people. He had for them a respect shared by the other Germanic and Gallic nations, by whom they were known as "the peculiar people of St. Peter and the church." Many times, at the solicitation of the pope, the Lombard monarch restored cities he had taken from the Roman and neighboring duchies, and his only open attack on Rome itself was due to the interference of the Romans in the business of his kingdom. The powerful duchies of Spoleto and Beneventum owed some allegiance to the Lombard monarch, but they were inclined to strike out for themselves. They had maintained what was practically an independence under the predecessors of Luitprand, but that king was not a man to brook insubordination, and he made his displeasure very plain to the rebellious dukes. Trasimund, duke of Spoleto, a proud and choleric soldier, braved the wrath of the none too patient Luitprand; and the Romans, perhaps with the notion that two powerful free duchies might act as a buffer between themselves and the enterprising barbarian warrior to the north, espoused his cause. Luitprand swept down on Spoleto, and Trasimund fled before the royal anger. He took refuge in Rome, and the Romans refused to surrender him to the monarch who followed swift upon his heels. Rebuffed by the people who had so often been the beneficiaries of his consideration, the Lombard king still refrained from attacking the Holy City, but he did seize four places in the northern part of the Roman division, and his soldiers pillaged the land up to the very walls of the city itself. Gregory III implored Luitprand to return the four towns, but the indignant Lombard refused to do so, and the pope appealed for aid to Charles Martel, the great king of the Franks.

THE BIRTH OF THE PAPAL STATE

This appeal, made in 739, was the first evidence of a change in the attitude of the Romans toward the old imperial system. Left to themselves in a hostile environment by a sovereign too weak to help them, they had helped themselves for a long period of years. In doing so they had made their agent not the impotent vicar of the civil government, but the bishop whose election made him their peculiar representative and whose religious position gave him advantages as a negotiator that none other could possess. But they still clung to the traditional form of government, although the real functions of government were otherwise exercised; just as to-day the City of London elects solemnly its lord mayor, a functionary without any function in the government of the municipality. They were Romans; the Byzantine emperor was the head of the Roman Empire; the rest of the world was barbarian. What there was of civilization they stood for; they sought to retain that distinction, and not to become the political province of a barbarian chief.

But now it was becoming apparent to the pope that the Byzantine hand was too weak to hold; that the Holy City was certain to be overrun by the barbarians unless protected by one of the barbarian powers. Reluctantly the Romans turned their faces from the East and looked for succor to the West. The religious sentiment was by no means an element in this reluctance. Indeed, between Rome and Byzantium there was division on religious matters, while the entire West was doctrinally at one with the pope.

The nuncios of Gregory III were received courteously at the court of the Frankish king, and Charles in return sent an embassy to the pope. But the time was not opportune for any hostile movement of the Franks against the Lombards. Luitprand and Charles were warm friends; more than that, they were military allies, the troops of the Lombard having rushed to join the Frankish warriors against the Saracens whose swords were gleaming in the fair fields of Provence. Besides that, Charles was quite convinced that while the Roman people might feel the wrath of Luitprand for their unwarranted interference in affairs that should not have concerned them, the head of the church and his clergy need fear no violence at the hands of the pious Lombard.

The Romans were left, therefore, to their own devices, and for the hour these devices did not fail them. With a flash of the ancient spirit and the ancient capacity, they armed and marched against the invaders, took Spoleto, and reinstated Trasimund on the ducal throne.

Luitprand, involved in numerous martial enterprises, took his time in preparation for the campaign against Beneventum, Spoleto, and Rome, but the whole peninsula was full of reports as to his purposes. While his sword was suspended above the devoted land, Pope Gregory died, following along the path to eternity Leo the Iconoclast and Charles Martel. Pope Zachary devoted the first days of his pontificate to safeguarding the future of the imperial city. He pointed out to his countrymen that the arms of the two duchies and the Byzantine provinces could hardly prevail over those of the mighty Lombard prince, to whom, after all, the Romans owed a debt of gratitude deeper than any they owed to his rebellious dukes.

The Romans accepted his counsel, and he went north to make peace with the king. His train was entirely ecclesiastical; it was made up of the robed priests of the church, and not of the armed soldiers of the empire. Luitprand, always loath to make war on the City of St. Peter, gladly accepted the Roman alliance and promised not to molest the Roman duchy. The troops of the *exercitus Romanus* joined him before Spoleto, and Trasimund surrendered unconditionally.

The Lombard king more than kept his promise to the pope. Not only did he restore to the Romans the four towns he had taken from them, but in the following year, when the Lombards invaded Ravenna and Zachary went to plead with the king on behalf of his neighbors, Luitprand good-naturedly gave up the conquered territory and ceased to molest the Ravennese.

In these years the pope appears as the defender of the imperial territory. Luitprand's successor, Ratchis, was as devoted to the See of St. Peter as the great king himself had been; and had he continued on the throne for long, there might have been a different history of Europe. Leaving Rome and Ravenna unmolested, he advanced against the imperial power at Pentapolis and Perugia, and was actually engaged in the siege of the latter place when Pope Zachary and his ecclesiastical train marched into the Lombard camp. Before the king the eloquent pope pleaded for peace; and so deep was the impression made by the pontiff on the mind of the Lombard chieftain that he not only withdrew his troops from the walls of Perugia, but took the crown from his brow and retired to a monastery to spend the remainder of his life in penitential exercises.

And now there came to rule over the plains of Lombardy a warrior given much less to piety and more to predation than either Ratchis or Luitprand, a crafty, ambitious leader who was convinced that the time had come to end forever the Byzantine domination over the Italian peninsula. Astolphus succeeded Ratchis in 749, and immediately took possession of Pentapolis and Ravenna. Under his ruthless heel the exarchate came to its end, and from the exarchal palace the Lombard king waved his sceptre over all of Italy between the Po and the Adriatic. In 752 Zachary died, and his successor, Stephen, found himself under the threat of a Lombard invasion. He at once sent ambassadors to his new and not desirable neighbor, and by them and him a treaty was negotiated under which Astolphus pledged himself to a peace of forty years' duration. His pledge held good for less than one-fortieth of the stipulated term, for in the autumn of the same year his troops were on the march, and halted only on the promise of a tribute of gold. The invader announced, further, that it was his purpose to cut Rome off from the empire and make the Holy City one of his dependencies.

Gloomy tidings, indeed, were these for the Roman people; to give up the glorious past; to lose that independence they had enjoyed under the weakening imperial system; to become vassals to strangers whose dress was wild, whose beards and hair were uncouthly shorn; to pass from political unity with civilization to political subordination to a barbaric power: all this it meant to a people proud of their peculiar position as citizens of a holy republic and heirs of the conquerors of the world. There was no division among them on this subject; the farmer and the tradesman shared with the duke and the pope the horror of such a situation.

For years the Romans had been pleading with the emperors to wake up to the dangers in the West, but the somnolent powers at Constantinople could not be awakened to the gravity of those dangers. At this juncture they did indeed take some slight notice of Pope Stephen's entreaties, and sent to Rome not armed legions, but John the Silentiary with letters to Astolphus and to the pope. The first was entreated to restore the territories of the empire he had annexed to his kingdom; the second to do what he could for the empire diplomatically. Stephen sent his brother Paul to Astolphus with the Byzantine ambassador, but the Lombard king was not much impressed by either the emperor's or the pontiff's representative. He did consent to send a messenger to Constantinople, but in the absence of that messenger he employed his time with incursions into the Roman duchy and the seizure of a castle or two.

Meanwhile the Romans were in a state of panic. With reason they expected little aid from the East, and in their distress they thought more often of a protectorate by the Frankish monarch under which they might continue to enjoy their independence. With this in view, the pope began a secret correspondence with Pepin, using as his messenger a peasant. He asked the Frank for a bodyguard to see him safely through Lombardy, as he desired to visit France. Pepin sent a Frankish bishop and the duke Auchtaire to escort him from Italy, and these, on their arrival in Rome, found John the Silentiary, who had returned from the Eastern court. The Byzantine had brought to Stephen a command of the emperor that he hold a personal interview with Astolphus and induce him to restore Ravenna to the empire.

Preceded by Auchtaire and escorted by his clerics and a splendid military company, Stephen set out for Pavia, the Lombard capital, to which Astolphus had retired from Ravenna. This was in October, 753. On the road the pontiff was met by a messenger from Astolphus with an entreaty that the pope refrain from any reference to the exarchy. It was an entreaty to which the pope paid scant respect, his diplomatic mission being to obtain the restoration of Ravenna. All his eloquence was wasted, however, although he was strongly backed by the imperial ambassador and by the Frankish nobles who stood at his side. The Lombard king would not concede an inch that he held by right of conquest, nor would he give any satisfactory guarantee with regard to his future proceedings.

The pope had made his last effort for the integrity of the Byzantine empire. It had demonstrated its weakness, and it was beyond his power to uphold its sovereignty longer against the rapacity of the Lombard. His business now was the protection of the "peculiar people" and their territory, and he went about the business without loss of time. Sending back to Rome the military escort, he proceeded, with his clerical entourage and his Frankish attendants, to the seat of the Frankish monarch. Pepin met him on the road and treated him with great respect and affection. To him Stephen made his plea, setting before him the state of Italy and the danger to the Roman republic, and begging him to protect the patrimony of Peter.

It was a plea that did not fall on deaf ears. The Frankish king was horrified at the idea of an attack by the Lombards on the headquarters of the Christian faith; he besought Astolphus through numerous ambassadors to refrain from such hostile activity and to refrain from the imposition of unaccustomed taxes. But Astolphus was stubborn; the entreaties of his Frankish neighbor did not move him, and Pepin swiftly took to the sword to effect what the tongue had been unable to bring about. At the head of his Frankish chivalry, he crossed into Italy, met Astolphus on the road, routed him, and pursued him to Pavia. Vanquished by the Western warriors, the Lombard king was compelled to yield back Ravenna and the other duchies, and Pepin sent the pope back to Rome, where the people received their pontiff with joyful acclamations.

Astolphus hardly waited until Pepin was back over the Alps before he laughed at his own promises and prepared to revenge himself on Rome. The pillage of the countryside by his outriders gave warning of the attack in force, and Rome had some time to prepare a defense against the three formidable columns of bearded men-at-arms whose weapons flashed in the sunshine outside her gates on New Year's morning of

756. All around the city the vengeful Lombard wasted the fields and villages, and again and again his charges threatened the very walls; but the Romans hurled back his storming parties, priests and abbots, with armor worn over their monastic robes, fighting with the lay soldiery on the ramparts. Meanwhile the pope smuggled his messengers by sea through the Lombard lines, and his appeals reaching Pepin at last, the king of the Franks and his terrible squadrons once more advanced into Italy in their war harness. Astolphus raised the siege of Rome to front his far more formidable foe. Step by step he was driven back until, cornered at last in Pavia, he was beaten again into submission.

Meanwhile some inkling of what was occurring in the West had penetrated the minds of the powers at Constantinople, and the victorious Pepin was met by a Byzantine ambassador who entreated him to restore Ravenna and the other duchies to the Eastern Empire. But the Frankish king shook his head; for St. Peter and the remission of his sins he had undertaken the war, he said, and on the shrine of St. Peter he proposed to lay the fruits of his victory. And he did as he said. At the head of a military division, the abbot Fulrad went with the Lombard commissioners from city to city, gathering the keys and hostages, and all these Fulrad took to Rome, depositing in the Confession of St. Peter the keys of the conquered cities together with the deed in which their conqueror made them over to the apostle and his successors.

Thus was the State of the Church born. All the circumstances of the time conspired to bring it about.

THE BIRTH OF THE PAPAL STATE

Under the protection of the Frankish monarch it was placed by the grateful pope, who bestowed upon Pepin the title of Patrician of the Romans. Other popes extended its confines, and not many years went by before there was revived the tradition of imperial protection, when Leo crowned Charlemagne emperor of the Romans and the Western Empire arose on the ruins of the Eastern.

This is a segment of the record of the progress of the church: not its spiritual progress so much as its temporal or material progress. What is it we see in it, now that we examine it closely? And what is it that others see? Draper, the Protestant historian, sees the cunning machinations of a perfectly organized priesthood; the triumph of a selfish, corrupt, superstitious, but marvellously subtle and politic priestcraft. By no other hypothesis can he account for the survival of the Roman Church—by no other hypothesis because the only alternative never suggests itself to his unconsciously but completely prejudiced mind.

Macaulay sees in a still greater segment something he cannot quite understand, but which compels, as he admits, his *reluctant* admiration. He accounts for it on the theory that "the polity of the Church of Rome is the very masterpiece of human wisdom." He speaks of the "forty generations of statesmen" whose experience gave perfection to that polity. But what made these popes statesmen? Many of them, before the time of which we treat, and after, were simple-minded religious enthusiasts, mortifying their flesh with haircloth shirts under the splendid pontifical vestments they wore. Many of them were the children of peasants and tradesmen who had graduated up through the priesthood to the primacy of the church. Was there really something else—something Macaulay could not see because of the traditions that had come down to him and the environment that affected even his enlightened mind?

What is there to see really, if we look at these things just as we look at political events of a more immediate past—the Spanish-American War, for instance, or the present seizure of Tripoli by the Italian government? Is there priestcraft reaching out for power? Or is there the picture of a world over which the system of law had broken down, an empire whose dead members, having sloughed off, became possessed of a new, fierce life and turned to rend the body from which natural decay had dissevered them? And in the midst of the bloody chaos is the human organization that holds the living light of a divine faith, and that turns this way and that, pleads and protests, gives blows and blessings, in a day-to-day struggle against the extinction of that light in the warring tides of ignorance and blood. And out of it all there comes the only thing that could come if darkness were not to swallow the world, as the Indians believe it does when the ecliptic shadow falls across the hills and valleys: a human state supporting the spiritual church, as the dark tower of rock supports the shining beam whose glory streams out over the troubled waters.

It was a state to vex sovereigns whose inclinations, otherwise unchecked by any law, were called to accountability here. It was a state against which they could rouse the race prejudice when religious constraint chafed their licentious spirits. It was something that was bound to have some of the corruption without which no human government has ever been, and to be open to attack therefor, and to a fierce arraignment in which a pinch of truth might be used to flavor an ocean of falsehood.

CHAPTER IV
THE MIDDLE AGES

THE mind that is accustomed to the contemplation of society's present form of political organization finds itself vexed by a study of the middle ages. We may say that now we deal in world politics with solids: Bosnia and Herzegovina may be severed from the Turkish Empire and become part of the Austrian, Tripolitania may be annexed to the Italian dominion, independent sovereignty may be ended in the Dutch republics of southern Africa to make them part of the British Empire, the Philippine Islands may be wrested from Spain and attached, more or less securely, to the American Union, but it is always a movement of pieces of things; it is like a breaking off and a sticking together of rigid substances. Unlike it altogether are the political changes of the middle ages. States seemed fluid then, or so slightly solidified that with amazing frequency and facility they were liquefied and disintegrated. There was a lack of stability; there was no fixity of territorial lines; Europe showed a kaleidoscopic political face. It was a huge, grotesque, magic countenance with changeable features, like one of its characteristic gargoyles whose nose wouldn't stay where it belonged. The Western emperor was not always of the same nationality, as had been for so long the case with the Romans and with the Greeks; sometimes he was a

Frank, sometimes a German, sometimes an Italian, sometimes a Lombard duke. A king might be vassal to a lesser lord or an ecclesiastical dignitary with regard to some of his provinces, or, it might be, only some of his castles, while with regard to the rest of his domain he owed allegiance to none. Law is to-day dependent ultimately upon force, but in those days it was more frankly and intimately dependent. A ruler was less likely to ask himself, "Have I a legal right?" than "Have I enough lances?" A vassal was more likely to ask, "May I safely rebel?" than "Must I legally obey?" Then further to obscure national lines came the crusades, the development of chivalry, the birth and growth of monastic military orders like the Templars and the Hospitallers, that spread a network of iron over all the nations of Christendom, exciting the fear and the jealousy of kings.

Yet underneath all this there was a uniform basis; throughout this strange society there was a universal influence, behind all this lawlessness there was law. The legal principle of the feudal constitution was that accountability was due to the source of power. It is the political legal principle to-day. The only difference is that the feudal lord never thought of the ultimate source, but only of the immediate source. If he held his fief from a duke, then it was to the duke he owed allegiance. If a pope bestowed a duchy on a Farnese, then were all the heirs and successors of that Farnese bound to render feudal service to the successors of that pope. If a king gave a province or a castle to a brave lance, then from that lance to that king, and from the successors of that lance to the successors of that king, was homage due. Nobody then thought of the people as the source of power—least of all the people themselves.

That was the principle of the political law of Europe in the middle ages, often violated but always recognized. Around that principle grew up a system of common law, and that system was animated and informed by the comprehensive influence of Christendom. Behind it was the coercive power of an unrecognized but potent public opinion which, united upon no other thing, was focalized upon the beneficial effect of a common religion. For this was the one thing that dignified the toiler of that age—his consciousness that he was a member of the church of God in common with all the toilers of all the Christian nations, and that between his helplessness and the absolute power of his lord that church interposed its moral code. It was the only institution in that day that opened its doors to him; every other path of advancement was barred to the lowly save that which led to St. Peter's chair, for peasant priests there were many and peasant popes were not infrequent. It was the only institution that made a place for the great mass; it was the visible and palpable embodiment of justice to a people who gave little thought to abstractions but hungered for material signs.

It is remarkable that in all the struggles between the church and the state in the middle ages, there is always something which concerns the rights of the common people. We can, for the present, leave to theologians the correctness of Boniface VIII's position in his long struggle with Philip the Fair of

France, but we will note among the causes for complaint urged by the pope against the king was the debasement of the coinage and the subsequent suffering of the common people. We read the long complaint of a German emperor against a pope with whom he was in conflict, and his reproach, "by the doing of which you have gained the applause of the vulgar." We see widows appealing to the church for justice against the rapacity of rulers; we see the abandoned and imprisoned wife of Philip Augustus appealing to the church against her royal husband; we see the wife of the imprisoned Richard of England urging the church to strike with the spiritual sword the faithless German emperor who had imprisoned her husband. Throughout Europe the confidence in the readiness of the church to defend the weak—who had no other defender then—was universal. And not only the peasant and the widow turned to the church in their distress: barons and princes and kings and emperors did likewise. Under the protection of St. Peter, the king about to embark on a crusade would leave his kingdom; against the ruthless power of a stronger neighbor a wronged duke would make complaint to the primate of the church. If two kings were at war and the arbitrament of the sword was unsatisfactory, the pope became the arbitrator, the justice of whose decree was assumed in advance.

The precedent of the coronation of Charlemagne as emperor of the West made it law that the pope should confirm the election of an emperor whose first duty was the protection of the church. The conferring of many of the estates of the church upon temporal rulers as fiefs of the church gave the pope by the law of the time a sovereignty that was political as well as spiritual over such estates. The voluntary assumption of feudal obligations by the rulers of other states made them, also, subject to the pope in a political way.

Meanwhile Christianity was working upon the moral constitution of the men who made up the world of the middle ages. It gave a noble tendency to the military enthusiasm of the day by teaching that gentleness was the obligation of the strong. It means something that then there came into English the title "gentle-man," applied, paradoxically, to those whose rude trade was war; every Romance language had an equivalent for that title. Knighthood received its sense of obligation from the church; at the altar of the Prince of Peace the youthful soldier prayed at the threshold of his career, clad in his robe of spotless white to symbolize the purity of his devotion; to the cause of Christ and his church he consecrated his virgin sword; to the succor of the weak and the defense of the widow and the orphan he pledged his lance by the oaths that the church prescribed. He must be brave and tender and truthful, he must keep his honor untarnished.

And these were the days of the torture-chamber! These were the days of private and public wars innumerable! These were the days when human life was held cheap not only by those who sought to take it, but often by those who parted with it laughingly.

At first blush we find it strange that the crimes recorded could have been so common in the days when devotion was so intense, when there was so passionate an idealism in the world. But it is not so strange. If there was one characteristic of the age, it seems to me that it was the utter lack of self-restraint. The power of self-constraint was intense; men would dare and *do* anything for an ideal, but it was another matter to refrain from doing. We read of Henry II of England chewing his lips until his mouth was covered with a bloody froth in his rage against Thomas à Becket. Frederick Barbarossa beat his head against the wall when unable to execute his whim, and wished that he, like Saladin, had no pope to vex him. Philip the Fair of France was not satisfied with the death of his papal enemy, but must drag him back from the grave to have him tried on monstrous charges which dead lips could not deny.

Possibly the best illustration of that devotion which found outlet in violent expression, but could not endure self-repression, is the letter the landgrave Philip of Hesse wrote to Melanchthon and the leaders of German Protestantism whose sanction to a divorce from his wife he begged. He made no charges against the lady at all. It was not difficult for him to establish his devotion to the cause of the Reformation—had he not given the last proof on many a sanguinary battle-field of his willingness to die for it?—but to live in fidelity to his marriage vows for more than a week at a time, for religion or anything else whatsoever, was simply impossible, so, please, he wanted a divorce. And the Protestant landgrave is only one of several such examples which may be summoned from the ghostly halls of history. Many a gallant Christian leader in earlier days, when there was no Protestant cause,

found it far more to his liking to fight for religion than
to live according to her precepts. Nearly all the causes
of quarrel between historical personages and the pope
had this element. The Catholic Philip Augustus and
the Protestant Henry VIII—if Henry can truly be
called a Protestant—found most irksome the matrimonial regulations of that church which one so vigorously defended with his sword and the other with his
pen. The valiant soldiers of the Cross who joyfully
undertook the hardships of distant travel and the
perils of war with a savage heathen foe, knelt in hu-
mility and devotion to receive the Substance of the
Lord from the hands of the priest on the morning of
battle, and then abandoned themselves to a blood-lust
that spared nothing human.

It is a marvellous age, an amazing time! We who
live in the security of civilized life, who carefully protect ourselves from every evil against which science
has devised a safeguard, whose faith is shallow and
whose dread of death is deep, find it hard to understand the men of that age so long gone by. They were
gay. The oppressed villein laughed in his miserable
bare hut; the outlaw laughed in Sherwood Forest
while his minstrel sang to him in humorous description of the gibbet on which he was likely to end his
mortal days; the rude baron, in his stone halls, drank
deep and laughed loud; the parish priest was cheery
and merry. It was in those days that England was
called "Merrie England." It was in those days that
the troubadours laughed at everything in their gay ir-
reverence, behind which there was perhaps a deeper
reverence than we know.

They were brave. If, in their superstition, ghostly things had terrors for them, actual death had none. They endured physical pain with a wonderful spirit: how it makes the heart beat to recall the one hundred and thirty knights of the condemned Temple Order who went to the fire in splendid procession, each looking upon death in its most frightful aspect with calm, contemptuous eyes, professing, as the flames wrapped his body round, his simple faith in the church whose priest had condemned him, and protesting the innocence of his great order! I sometimes think that it was more because of the heroic temper of the men of that age than because of their cruelty that the torture became a part of the judicial process. To-day simple death is sufficient to inspire fear in the mind of man; then something more terrifying than death had to be employed.

They were violently virtuous. Their penances were real; not the mere recitation of prayers, not the simple mental humiliation satisfied the penitent—an emperor of Germany stands for three bitter days in the snow at the gate of a church, shivering in the bitter blast, to gain the pardon of the offended priest of God. Thousands leave their castles and their fertile fields, their servants and their families, to go on foot, by roads infested with robber bands, through countries strange in speech and custom, and at last in creed, penniless and in poor garb, in order to gain the forgiveness of God.

But if violently virtuous, they are also violently evil —in all things they are violent. The rage of Sciarra Colonna drives his mailed fist at the triple-crowned head of the venerable vicar of Christ; the rude clutch of William de Nogaret plucks the primate of Christendom from the throne of Peter and hurls the aged but indomitable prelate, feeble in body because of his eighty-six years, but strong in mind and spirit still, among the hired banditti who did the will of Philip of France at Anagni.

What thought a ruler then of the rights of subjects? Who among the kings and dukes cared a snap of his fingers for abstract right and wrong where his passions were engaged? What was the state? Was it an organization for the public good? Who dreamed, in state affairs, of the public good? What were the political questions of the day? The amours of a king. The question of the marriage of his son or his daughter. The divorce of his wife. The support of his mistress. The assassination of his rival. The extortion of money from his people. The robbery of his neighbors. Adultery, murder, robbery—these were the political questions of the middle ages; these were the matters upon which monarchs claimed independence of the popes.

And what was the state? Was it not what Louis XIV declared it to be in his famous "L'Etat c'est moi"? Government was personal, national welfare meant the aggrandizement of the monarch, the feeding fat of his hunger for wealth and power and glory. The King of France called himself "France," and addressed his brother monarch as "England." When a German ruler said, "We are dealing with Aragon," what he meant, and what everybody knew he meant, was that *he* was dealing with *Ferdinand*. Rulers called themselves "we."

What would have been the result if these rulers, each intent upon his own satisfaction, had imposed always their own whims upon those subject to them? What would have fallen upon the world if the absolute freedom from responsibility they craved had been freely granted them? What if there had been nothing to oppose their selfish violence; no force in all Europe to say them nay? If you consider what they were and what they knew, how strong were their bodies, how fearless their spirit, how fierce their pride, how headlong and ruthless their violence, what picture does your mind reflect of a world left to their mercies?

Against this violence, this fierce and passionate self-assertion, stood the philosophy and the teaching of the church. Against the idea of the irresponsibility of kings stood the church doctrine of the accountability of all human creatures, kings and subjects, princes and peasants, for their moral conduct. Again and again the prelates of the church declared, when none else was so bold as to declare it, that he was no king who ruled unjustly and wickedly, but a tyrant. The passion of the day was war: the church preached peace among the Christian nations. The selfishness of power demanded slavery: the church preached that no Christian should be a chattel. The church set its ban upon trial by ordeal. It preached self-restraint, and its servants banded themselves into societies where self-restraint might be practised as an example and an expiation. With a rigid moral code that was practical and precise in detail it checked the licentiousness of the age, and I use the word *licentiousness* in the most comprehensive sense.

TWO AND TWO MAKE FOUR

In the collision of the two psychological forces, the savage and the civilized, the licentious and the lawful, occurred those things which have shocked historical precisians who fail to perceive the vast difference between writing a law and getting men to live by it. The church's moral power was backed by physical power. The very passionate objective expression of the age that made the control of temporal rulers difficult, furnished material weapons for the pope. If there was a de Nogaret, with a heart of fierce hate, to pull the pope down, there were thousands of proud warriors ready and eager with as fierce a devotion to exalt him. Colonna's mercenaries thrust the aged Boniface into prison; the armed peasantry stormed the prison walls to set him free. The savage Roman barons drove the pope from Rome, and the Norman warriors fiercely put the Romans to the sword in restoring the pontiff to his seat.

Here on two sides, then, were there directing and compelling forces of the same nature bearing in upon the rebellious inclinations of temporal powers. The Christian peoples, including the lower as well as the upper orders, and even the kings themselves when their desires were not opposed and their selfish passions not engaged, made the law of the church their law. It had been so from the age of Theodosius, the moral precepts of the church had been written into the imperial statutes. More and more it became so in western Europe—naturally, necessarily. To whom did all these people of the West look for inspiration and moral law? Was it not the church? How could it have been possible for a generation so headlong in its devotion to form a system of laws that was not, in all that then seemed to them virtuous and just, based upon and in perfect harmony with the precepts of that institution that men—even those who fought it—believed to be of divine inspiration and divine authority? "Men then believed their form of faith," says John W. Draper, and no more bitter critic of the Roman Catholic Church ever wrote, "with the same clearness, the same intensity, with which they believed their own existence or the actual presence of things upon which they cast their eyes. The doctrines of the church were to them no mere inconsequential affair, but an absolute, an actual reality, a living and a fearful thing." And such men, so believing, were bound under the laws of human nature to make the civil reinforce the ecclesiastical law. So we find that not only infractions of the moral code, as it is to-day universally understood, but violations of the church law were prohibited by the civil statutes. The law of the empire as well as the law of the church made heresy a crime; the church punished it with the spiritual sword, the civil government with the stake and the gibbet. Rulers deemed it dangerous to the state that heresy should spread among the people: they left the determination of what was heresy to the theologians, but the punishment they took into their own hands. The only punishment the church ever inflicted on John Huss was spiritual: his doctrines were declared to be heretical, and he was stripped of his vestments and degraded from the priestly office. His execution, *for a crime against the civil law*, was the act of the emperor. These were the words in which the Council of Constance dismissed his case: "Since Holy Church has nothing more to perform in the case of John Huss, this Holy Synod of Constance decrees that he be delivered to the secular judgment and the secular power."

Professor Draper and many other historians have laid upon the shoulders of the church all the atrocities of the time, but historical research confirms what common sense would conclude, that an institution depending for general recognition of its divine character upon an ideal could not have been steeped in crimes that even that violent age abhorred. In such research, according to the editors of the *Cambridge Modern History*, "the honest student finds himself continually deserted, retarded, misled by the classics of historical literature, and has to hew his own way through multitudinous transaction periodicals and official publications in order to reach the truth." The same authorities state that "the long conspiracy against the revelation of the truth has gradually given way." I think they are wrong in assuming it to be a conspiracy. No doubt many a historian wrote atrocious falsehoods as facts, not because he conspired against the truth, but because he believed his falsehoods to be facts. He depended on what "everybody knows." My theory with regard to it is this: Throughout Europe, and especially among the common people, there was the same idea with regard to persons in official life that prevails among Americans to-day. Superstition was prevalent; men believed in speaking heads, in witches, in a hundred other absurdities. Among the superstitious peoples, and particularly those of northern Europe, all sorts of stories passed current—stories of kings and knights and bishops and popes. The accusations that an emperor in his wrath would hurl at a pontiff sifted down to the peasantry in every exaggerated form and became a part of the inn-yard gossip in many a distant province. Often, changed marvellously in the telling, they persisted long after the emperor and the pontiff had forgotten them—indeed, long after emperor and pontiff had appeared at the bar of a Higher Judge—and generation passed them on to generation. We have evidence in America of a Maine farmer who for nearly ninety years voted for Andrew Jackson for President.

All this tavern gossip, all the countryside scandals, the first preachers of the Reformation gathered together, adding it to the abuses acknowledged to exist in the organization of the church. The plots of Boccaccio's lewd jokes, the subject of the jongleur's irreverent ballads—these were seriously put forward as proven facts, and a not too inquisitive Protestant advocacy so accepted them. And so they came down to the Protestant writers of conventional history, and from them they came down to us. Draper, for instance, lays the blame of the sack of Constantinople by the crusaders on the church, although quoting Pope Innocent's indignant protest against the enormities of that pillage. The church is held up as responsible for the cruelties even of those Christian princes with whom she was constantly in trouble because of her refusal to remain silent in the face of their public offenses against the moral law. The soldiers she employed were often cruel: the soldiers of that excessive age were nearly always cruel. They liked to smite with the sword, and they found it comfortable to believe that they might smite without scruple when they smote an enemy of Christ. A bias in favor of our own frailties is not so rare in this age that we should not expect to find it in other ages. There are men to-day who can pray and prey at the same time; is it odd that such existed in the earlier generations? The false conscience is not peculiar to this day of the world. But it was no more encouraged by the Christian church, as far as the record runs, in the middle ages than it is to-day. But because soldiers were cruel, why should the church, whose constant preaching was in favor of mercy, be held responsible? Does common sense to-day hold responsible for the ferocious conduct alleged of the soldiers of the Italian king in Tripoli, the Pope of Rome, simply because the king is a Christian king and he has appealed to the old crusading sentiment of Europe by announcing his purpose of "planting the Cross in Tripoli"?

We have said that there were two forces of the same nature bearing in upon the law-making civil powers. One such force was public opinion. The people of that time willed it that the law of the church should be their law. Why did they so will it? Let Professor Draper answer—a prejudice in favor of the church will never be alleged of him. After indicting and convicting of every crime imaginable a long succession of the pontiffs, laying at their doors impurity, licentiousness, blood-guilt, simony, blasphemy, and atheism, he concludes a chapter on "The European Age of Faith" thus:

"But there is another, a very different aspect, under which we must regard this church. Enveloped as it was with the many evils of the time, the truly Christian principle which was at its basis perpetually vindicated its power, giving rise to numberless blessings in spite of the degradation and wickedness of man. As I have elsewhere remarked: 'The civil law exerted an exterior power in human relations; Christianity produced an interior and moral change. The idea of an ultimate accountability for personal deeds, of which the old Europeans had an indistinct perception, became intense and precise. The sentiment of universal charity was exemplified, not only in individual acts the remembrance of which soon passes away, but in the more permanent institution of establishments for the relief of affliction, the spread of knowledge, the propagation of truth. Of the great ecclesiastics, many had risen from the humblest ranks of society, and these men, true to their democratic instincts, were often found to be the inflexible supporters of right against might. Eventually coming to be the depositaries of the knowledge that then existed, they opposed intellect to brute force, in many instances successfully, and by example of the organization of the church, which was essentially republican, they showed how representative systems may be introduced into the state. Nor was it over communities and states that the church displayed her chief power. Never in the world before was there such a system. From her central seat at Rome, her all-seeing eye, like that of Providence itself, could equally take in a hemisphere at a glance or examine the private life of any individual.

Her boundless influences enveloped kings in their palaces and relieved the beggar at the monastery gate. In all Europe there was not a man too obscure, too insignificant, or too desolate for her. Surrounded by her solemnities, every one received his name at the altar; her bells chimed at his marriage, her knell tolled at his funeral. She extorted from him the secrets of his life at her confessionals, and punished his faults by her penances. In his hour of sickness and trouble her servants sought him out, teaching him by her exquisite litanies and prayers to place his reliance on God, or strengthening him for the trials of life by the example of the holy and the just. Her prayers had an efficacy to give repose to the souls of his dead. When, even to his friends, his lifeless body had become an offense, in the name of God she received it into her consecrated ground, and under her shadow he rested till the great reckoning-day. From little better than a slave she raised his wife to be his equal, and, forbidding him to have more than one, met her recompense for those noble deeds in a friend at every fireside. Discountenancing all impure love, she put around that fireside the children of one mother, and made that mother little less than sacred in their eyes. In ages of lawlessness and rapine, among people but a step above savages, she vindicated the inviolability of her precincts against the hand of power, and made her temples a refuge and a sanctuary for the despairing and oppressed. Truly, she was the shadow of a great rock in many a weary land!' "

We can readily see how in this age, when nations are sharply defined and their populations, nationally

united, are denominationally divided in countless
Christian and non-Christian religious and anti-religious organizations, it is utterly impracticable to
make the laws of any one church the laws of a state.
But in the time of which Draper speaks, and under the
conditions he describes, can common sense conceive
of any other possibility than the insistence of the people upon civil laws in consonance with the precise
precepts of such an institution? Surely in a day when
enlightened opinion is all on the side of the correctness of the democratic principle of government, it will
not be held that the nations of Christendom had not
then the right to demand such laws as they desired,
nor in the face of the testimony of such fierce Protestants as Draper can it be said that their desire for the
laws of the church was unwise. They say that the
pragmatic philosophy, the philosophy that judges by
results, is the philosophy of modern America. Judged
by even that philosophy, was the impregnation of civil
law with religious precept in the middle ages correct
in principle? Again let Draper tell us. "Europe had
made a vast step during its Age of Faith," he says in
his *Intellectual Development of Europe.* "Sponta-
neously, it had grown through its youth; and the
Italians, who had furnished it with many of its ideas,
had furnished it also with many of its forms of life.
In that respect justice has still to be done them. When
Rome broke away from her connections with Constantinople, a cloud of more than Cimmerian darkness
overshadowed Europe. It was occupied by wander-
ing savages. Six hundred years organized it into
families, neighborhoods, cities. Those centuries found

it full of bondmen; they left it without a slave. They found it a scene of violence, rapine, lust, they left it the abode of God-fearing men. Where there had been trackless forests there were innumerable steeples glittering in the sun; where there had been bloody chieftains, drinking out of their enemies' skulls, there were grave ecclesiasts fathoming the depths of free-will, predestination, election. Investing the clergy with a mysterious superiority, the Church asserted the equality of the laity, from the king to the beggar, before God. It disregarded wealth and birth and opened a career for all."

Truly, the world to-day might well wish for a new Age of Faith!

The other force of which I have spoken was the international law of the day. The common consent of nations gave the pope a position among the princes such as the lovers of peace are now trying to establish for the Hague Tribunal. Kings made appeal to him, and the legality of his decree was universally recognized. In the light of this simple fact there is nothing astonishing in the bulls which are held up as proof of the hunger of the papacy for temporal power. To say, as historians have said, that the church divided the world between Spain and Portugal gives such an impression as that, surely; but how the impression fades in the mind when we examine the bulls themselves and the circumstances in which they were issued, when we know that the two kings of those two estates appealed to the pope, not for territory, but for an arbitration of certain counterclaims between them. Then these bulls appear to us as merely the judgment of an arbitrator called on to pass on the merits of a controversy, intended to prevent conflict between two great exploring powers over territories they might discover, and not over lands already occupied, the rights of whose princes are expressly asserted in the bull.

I have tried briefly to picture the age, its thought, its custom, its law. Judging it upon such facts as are readily accessible, upon the testimony of Protestant as well as Catholic historians, and in the light of ordinary common sense, it seems to me that church law was civil law because the people of the time wanted it so to be; that the political activities of the popes were due to their peculiar position in the world of that day, and to the wish of the rulers themselves; that voluntary devotion gave them material power as well as spiritual authority; and finally that the personal character of government made the acts of government for the most part the moral acts of individuals for which they as individuals were accountable to God, whose vicar they believed the Bishop of Rome to be. As I have said, the political acts of the time were very often just plain adultery, murder, and robbery, and surely such things come within the sphere of the spiritual authority. It may be true that in that violent hour, when kings dealt out rude blows with the mailed fist to the very person of the pontiff, and thousands of swords were ready to write that pontiff's decrees in letters of blood upon the domain of his enemy, the ecclesiastical may have at times infringed upon the domain of the civil power. But if the pope overstepped the limit, the secular ruler overstrode it; the

whole history of the time seems an effort on the part
of sovereigns to subject religion to their interests,
to make it international in its influence with respect to
their neighbors, but strictly national with respect to
dependence upon and control by themselves. What is
all the battle about investitures? Is it not the struggle of the church to free itself from the enforced
nomination of its episcopal dignitaries by the kings
and emperors? In these days and in this country we
well know the meaning of *patronage.* The word itself
comes from those times and those countries: the kings
made the episcopal offices of the church the patronage
of the crown. The effect of their policy, which the
church always resisted, was to make the bishops less
priests than princes, less servants of the church than
ministers of the king. What was the object of Philip
the Fair? Was it not to make a church universal in
its influence, but French in its inspiration and allegiance; to turn to his own earthly account the powers
that should be exercised, as they had been delegated,
only for the kingdom of God?

The hour has long gone by. The world is not the
same world; the state is not now, nor can it ever again
be, in its political significance, some single soul using
a nation as his footstool. We have looked back to that
time when we are given to believe there was a pernicious union of church and state. We haven't found
what there was pernicious; nay, more, we haven't
found any state. None, surely, that corresponds to
the meaning *state* has to us in this generation.

Will there ever be such an hour again? Will that
knighthood ever again ride in iron harness the lonely

marches, from castle to castle, from walled town to walled town? When it does, and when among the nations of the earth, or in any one of them, there is the uniformity of religious belief that then bound Christendom in a common faith, instead of the diversity that now sunders it into countless creeds, perhaps those who dread a union of church and state may have a cause for such dread. But not until then.

CHAPTER V

GREGORY THE "POLITICIAN"

TRUTH is irrepressible. No matter what may be the prejudice of the man who knows it, he cannot suppress it in his breast. It will break through, fighting for place with the falsehoods his venom may invent or his prejudice project. And common sense is capable generally of recognizing the truth and the falsehood, if common sense be allowed full play and be not blinded by preconceptions. That is our safety in this age. Not all of us have the time to search out the hidden original documents in which the editors of the *Cambridge Modern History* and other historians say the truth lies; indeed, such can be the task of only a few, so that the mind of the world must be influenced by the popular histories. But a little practical common sense, such as we exercise with regard to business affairs, will protect us against many errors. The occupations of my own life have excluded such an engrossing search as would make me *know* the details of life in remote ages; but with what my common sense can make of such materials as conventional history furnishes, I have been able to reach conclusions which later have been confirmed by the views of men of profound scholarship. In another place I advanced, for instance, a theory with regard to the effect of medieval tavern gossip upon the minds of Protestant advocates and historians. Imagine my

surprise to find my view of the matter confirmed by
no less an authority than Martin Luther. *"In the
taverns,"* wrote Luther, "people vied with one another in relating amusing anecdotes about the ava-
rice of priests. The keys, the power of the popes, etc.,
were there also ridiculed." How much of what has
colored our minds with respect to the Catholic Church
comes from such a source; how much of it rolled
originally off the thick tongue of the bar-room wit?
For example, that story of the female pope which,
Macaulay says in his essay on Gladstone's *Church and
State,* "has been disproved by the strict researches of
modern criticism," although, as he informs us in the
same sentence, it was "once believed throughout all
Europe." I have heard it often from good members
of Protestant churches who accepted it as established
historical fact, and who had never noticed the ten
words in which Macaulay announced its falsity. Yet
their common sense would have branded the story as
falsehood if a prejudice colored by many another
similar tale had not hampered its operations. Another
widely circulated myth that affects the Protestant
mind is the story of the pope who excommunicated a
comet. The story originated very naturally. A great
comet, sweeping into our field of vision as it made the
huge circuit of its celestial orbit, alarmed the peoples
of Europe, and they had recourse to prayer for preser-
vation from a menace no human power could resist.
The world hasn't changed so much, in so far as fundamental human nature is concerned; the last visit of
the Halley comet, and the vagueness of scientific
opinion with regard to the possibility of a collision in

the wide reaches of space, caused much the same hysteria in our own generation. The pope, by public prayer, endeavored to soothe the frightened people. The comet flashed through the sky and went its way; the hysteria found relief in laughter. Now it is quite likely that at that very time thousands of ignorant peasants in the remoter parts of Europe believed that the pope had excommunicated the comet. The humor of the thing appealed to some; others took the story quite seriously: it was their mental tribute to the power and courage of the vicar of Christ. The popes had hurled their curses at mighty kings and proud emperors: to the mind of the ignorant serf, why should he falter before the flaming devil who dominated the sky? And so our historians have gone again for their facts, not to the written record, but to the folk-lore of an ignorant peasantry. A future generation may laugh at us, as we laugh at the generations gone by, when historians, after reading the files of our newspapers of the spring of 1910, write down that science predicted a collision of the earth and the comet and the annihilation of the human race by a whisk of its radiant tail; and that all the world giggled at the learned astronomers on the morning of the nineteenth of May because those wonderful gentlemen had lost the tail of the comet and, like little Bo-Peep, didn't know where to find it.

I find some passages in history that ring true to me; my common sense accepts the evidence adduced; I find analogies in the life of the world of to-day, in the facts of common human experience. And the man for whom I am writing this, the man in the street, who

of Christendom—for even then there were piety and purity in the body of the church—were gathering together to protect it against the evil results of political domination. The foes they had to face might well daunt men of a less lofty courage and purpose. In Rome was a corrupt aristocracy, bent upon recovering the control of the papacy from the German power, not in order that it might be purified, but in order that it might be made to minister to their pleasure and profit. In Germany were warrior kings of vaulting ambition and unbridled passions, supported by a political clergy who had disregarded the ancient canonical rule of celibacy and lived scandalous lives. Along the coast were the Saracen ships threatening the Italian towns. If, as conventional history asserts, it was a political purpose that animated these priests, strange was the political wisdom that could foresee a victory over a combination such as this. The cunning priestcraft of pagan lands ever sought the support of power; but this amazing priestcraft defied human power, pitting itself recklessly against a brutal empire, an intrenched aristocracy, a corrupted clerical force of great numerical strength; against men of power and what they loved; against not only the political strength, but the long-established evils that had all the force and tenacity of common custom; against the *fashion* of the day. Has the world ever seen *cunning* like this? "Forty generations of statesmen," says Macaulay. What remarkable *statesmanship!*

The Roman chiefs were the first to feel the rigor of the reform, and they took characteristic measures to combat it. Stephen IX, although they had elected him, had disappointed them; they had him poisoned as he travelled in Tuscany. Immediately they called an election and placed Benedict X on the papal throne. But the clergy took no part in the election; they denounced it as illegal and in violation of the oath the Romans had taken when Stephen IX set out on his journey, that they would elect no pope until Hildebrand was among them, in the event of Stephen's death, which he seems to have expected. Aided by a noble of the Trastevere—Leo, the son of a converted Jew—they fled from Rome and gathered around Hildebrand. He at once assembled a conclave which elected Nicholas II, who was installed in St. Peter's chair on January 24, 1059; Benedict X having departed hurriedly upon the approach of Leo's men-at-arms. Hildebrand overcame the objection of the German emperor to the election of Nicholas, and when the Romans rebelled and again elevated Benedict, he called upon the Normans who were establishing themselves on the coast, and with the help of those remarkable warriors subdued the city aristocracy and ejected the pretender to the pontificate. Then came that great council at which Hildebrand freed the church. It made the rule that the right of the election of the pope should lie in the hands of the cardinal bishops.

Hildebrand knew very well what that meant. He knew the interests that would be antagonized, and against those interests he sought to protect the church. He found his weapons for the material conflict in the Norman settlements of the south. In those formidable warriors he found the simplicity and devotion he needed, and he took advantage of the feudal law of the times to make them vassals of the church. In the Council of Melfi, on August 23, 1059, the church bestowed on the Norman chiefs, Richard and Robert Guiscard, the principality of Capua and the duchy of Apuleia and Calabria, and in return the two captains took the oath of military service.

Throughout the years that followed the German emperors exercised the powers of confirmation which the council had reserved to them, and when, in 1073, the clergy insisted upon elevating to the pontificate the son of the Tuscan carpenter who had already done so much toward its regeneration, it is a strange letter that Hildebrand sends to the emperor Henry IV. He hopes his election will be set aside, and he candidly informs the emperor that if chosen as pope he will call him to account for the scandal of his conduct. Strange politician is this!

Once in the papal chair, he "addressed himself to tear out every vestige of simony and concubinage with a remorseless hand," as Draper puts it. The pious countess Beatrice and her daughter Matilda ruled Tuscany, and Gregory wrote to them, urging them to hold no communion with bishops who had bought their offices. His legates went into Germany, deposing bishops whose dignities had been purchased from the emperor. Henry sold the see of Milan to Godfrey, but the stern pope put down the king's bishop from his seat. In Rome justice is done to the brutal and vicious lords, and they seek alliance with the German. One of them, at the instigation of the emperor, breaks into the Church of St. Mary, followed by a band of bravos, on Christmas night, and the pontiff is torn from the altar, wounded, and carried a prisoner to the castle of the Cenci. Throughout the city the alarm runs—sacrilege has been done; the beloved pontiff is in the hands of his enemies! Bells are rung from the churches, the tradesmen, the laborers, the great population of Rome, throng the streets. Cencis finds a shrieking multitude swirling around his castle; his men-at-arms are as nothing against this furious horde; they bring ladders and scale the walls; they put the bravos to the blade and storm through the captured stronghold until they find the wounded but undismayed pope. The conspirators flee from Rome.

And now Henry gathers around him the political bishops of Germany, and at Worms he assembles a council before whom he lays charges against Gregory. His ecclesiastical henchmen do his will; they pass a decree declaring the pope deposed. Their decree the emperor sends to Gregory with a letter full of abuse. In Rome the pope assembles the Lateran Council, and against the emperor he launches the curse of the church. The German monarch is laid under an interdict: Christians are bound no longer by their oath of allegiance to him; no longer is he king, but tyrant, and the "power to bind and loose" has been exercised to free them from subjection to a wicked sovereign.

And now Henry was to learn how well Hildebrand had done his work in all the preceding years. The priests of Gregory went throughout Germany, publishing the papal decree. The people shrank away from an accursed king, and many of the princes seized the opportunity to wreak private vengeance for wrongs long suffered. A council of the electors was held and Rudolph of Swabia chosen in Henry's place by the princes.

In terror of the rising storm, Henry sought a reconciliation with the possessor of so terrible a power. In midwinter he crossed the Alps and sought out Gregory in Canossa. But the mere promise of peace would not satisfy the pope. Henry must give evidence of penance for his sins. There was the snow-covered and wind-swept portal of the church, there should the proud king humble himself, fasting and praying in the cold, before he might be reconciled with the church he had outraged. And when his ordeal was over and the aged pontiff celebrated the mass at which Henry was to be admitted to communion, Gregory lifted the chalice and called upon God to strike him dead as he stood if he were guilty of the charges the monarch had made against him, and dared the guilty king to do as he had done. Henry shrank back.

But he had accomplished his purpose, no matter how bitter a humiliation it had cost him. The interdict was lifted, he was free, his vassals would come again to his call. He gathered them round him and took the field against Rudolph, who was wounded in battle and died of his wounds. Henry soon felt himself strong enough to gratify his hatred of Gregory, who had never conferred upon him the imperial crown. He summoned a council of clerical enemies of the pope, and had Gilbert, the excommunicated bishop of Ravenna, proclaimed as pope. With his

army he marched on Rome in 1081. The countess
Matilda and Beatrice, her mother, gave his troops
battle, but he managed to take Rome in 1084. The
Roman aristocrats made his entrance easy and wel-
comed him joyfully, hoping for a return of the old
times and the régime of a pope under whom licentious
conduct and rapine would not be severely punished.
Gregory, who had solemnly excommunicated Henry,
shut himself up in the Castle of St. Angelo. The martial countess of Tuscany, in her efforts to relieve him,
inflicted severe reverses on the imperial troops in
Lombardy, but it remained for the Norman captain,
Robert Guiscard, to rescue the pontiff from the hands
of his adversaries. Although well advanced on a
career of conquest in the Byzantine dominions, Guiscard never hesitated when he heard of the pope's
perilous situation. He hastened with all speed back to
Italy, and his knights were soon sweeping down upon
the imperial forces at Rome. Alarmed at the approach of this terrible antagonist, Henry withdrew his
troops; but the Roman aristocrats could not willingly
relinquish their hope of a period of license, and they
denied the Normans entry to the city. Robert
stormed the walls and put them to the sword. Fearing to leave the pope in Rome, he took him with him
to the abbey of Monte Cassino, and later to Salerno.
In that city, in 1088, died this strange *politician*, whose
last words were: "I have loved justice and hated wickedness, and therefore I die in exile." Statesman?
Draper calls the works of Machiavelli "the purest example we possess of physical statesmanship." Count
de Maistre describes them as a treatise on "How shall

assassins outwit one another?" Then Gregory's statesmanship was not *physical statesmanship.* "I have loved justice and hated wickedness": there is nothing like that in Machiavelli.

Again I look at a period of church history and see only what is there to be seen. It isn't design, it isn't cunning, it isn't priestcraft. It is simply this: Hildebrand's endeavors in behalf of a free and pure Christianity ran counter to the pleasure of Henry, who wished to sell bishoprics, and, with a brutal and ignorant autocrat's fierce anger at anything that dared to call him to account for sins that shocked the world, he tried to beat down what he could not control.

Rapidly I shall pass over the events of the period intervening between the reign of Henry IV and the time of that Frederick of whom Voltaire speaks. In that period succeeding emperors had attacked the papacy in an effort to make the church political. In that period a Henry had helped the Duke of Austria rob and imprison the returning crusader, Richard the Lion-hearted, and had been called to account by the pope, under whose protection were all crusaders on the roads to and from the Holy Land. In that period Henry VI had fought for the ancient power of the emperors over the bishoprics and had lost, dying reconciled to the church. In that period Frederick Barbarossa had boasted, "I am the lord of the world," and "The will of the ruler is law," only to admit, after a short conflict, that there was a higher law and to spend the remainder of his glorious reign in peace with the church.

And now came the second relentless foe of the

popes, the able, crafty, infidel Lord of the Sicilies, who dreamed of an empire of vast extent subject to his despotic sceptre alone, who had as little patience with opposition as Napoleon was to exhibit in later times, and, like Napoleon, saw in the papacy little more than an instrument to be used to cement his power. Frederick II was not, like many of his predecessors, a mere ignorant freebooter with an imperial title. Little of his time was spent in Germany; his youth and most of his manhood he passed in the more enlightened cities of Italy. The son of Henry VI, he had been protected after his father's death by the very power he was soon to assail. As an orphan child he had been safeguarded from the Emperor Otto by Pope Innocent III. He was instructed in all the arts and the science of the day. Heir to the kingdom of Sicily, he passed his youth in conversation with learned men. As he grew into manhood he showed a predilection for Mohammedan associates and Jewish and Moslem instructors. "To his many other accomplishments," Draper says, "he added the speaking of Arabic as fluently as a Saracen. He delighted in the society of Mohammedan ladies, who thronged his court. His enemies asserted that his chastity was not improved by association with these miscreant beauties. The Jewish and Mohammedan physicians and philosophers taught him to sneer at the pretensions of the church. From such ridicule it is but a short step to the breaking off of authority. At this time the Spanish Mohammedans had become widely affected with irreligion; their greatest philosophers were infidel in their own infidelity."

[96]

This was not an influence likely to incline the policy of Henry in accord with the spirit of the militant Christendom of the day. For the crusades had been preached—by Peter the Hermit and Walter the Penniless Europe had been roused to rescue the tomb of the Saviour from the hand of the unbeliever. Urban II and Innocent III had, by virtue of their office, taken the lead in the Christian movement. Frederick knew well the spirit of the time, and, while not in sympathy with it, did not hesitate to use it. He was well aware that no one not believed to be heart and soul in the project of the reclamation of the Holy Land could attain to the imperial dignity, and he was prodigal of promises. His first promise was to give the kingdom of Sicily to his son as a kingdom distinct from Germany, for Sicily was a fief of the church and its political union with Germany would complicate the relationships of the Pontifical State. He took up the Cross, and declared himself among the most enthusiastic of the soldiers of the faith. His tardiness in setting forth against the infidel and in keeping his promise with regard to the Sicilian succession after he had received the German monarchical crown, embittered the last days of Innocent III, his guardian; but he made such professions of future conduct to Honorius III, and was so emphatic in his promise to begin a campaign against the paynim immediately, that that pontiff gave him the imperial crown at Rome on November 22, 1220.

It must be remembered that the law of the time made the emperor, primarily, the soldier of the church. That was the law of the creation of the Western Empire. The knighthood of Europe looked to the pope to give it in the emperor a leader in the Holy War. Damietta, for which the Christians had paid a bitter price in blood, was taken from them in 1219, and upon its fall there came from the masters of the crusading orders who held the Christian frontier, and from the patriarch of Jerusalem, letters of reproach to the pope for his failure to send the emperor to their relief. Honorius, grieved by the loss to the cause, wrote to Frederick in 1221 reminding the emperor of his promises. Frederick, who was very busy extending his own dominions, even to the prejudice of the States of the Church, replied with fresh promises. His marriage to Yolande de Lusignan, daughter of the King of Jerusalem, gave the pope a fleeting hope, but Frederick extinguished it by applying to his father-in-law to get him excused from crusade service until he had subdued the Lombards. At last the pope sent to Frederick two cardinals who were directed to bring the matter to an issue, and at San Germano in July, 1225, Frederick signed a solemn undertaking to embark in the crusade within two years; swearing that if he fulfilled not his promise he should be driven from the communion of the church, and that his person and his dominions should, by a just judgment, be at the disposition of the pope.

Honorius died in 1227, and Gregory IX succeeded him in St. Peter's chair. It is quite likely that the new pope entertained little hope of any real activity on Frederick's part, although the emperor seemed to yield at last to the threat of excommunication and marched toward southern Italy. The vigorous Gregory had assembled a fine army of crusaders, and it looked as if at last the hopes of Christendom might be realized. But Frederick had no real design of attacking his Mohammedan friends; three days after his departure he was back again in Italy, to the bitter disappointment of the pope. The splendid body of soldiery melted away and Frederick retired to take the baths at Pozzuoli.

The period of probation fixed by Frederick himself came to a close, and the pope pronounced his excommunication in September, 1227. Frederick scoffed at the action of the pope, and published attacks upon the character of Gregory. In all the empire he played the freebooter, robbing the crusading orders, and maintaining his dissolute court crowded with Saracen women and infidel preachers. In 1228 Gregory held a synod in Rome and repeated the excommunication. The adherents of Frederick among the Roman aristocracy raised a revolt in the city and drove the pope from his palace. Meanwhile Frederick at last started for the Holy Land, on what he was pleased to call his crusade.

It was an odd crusade. "The Christian camp," Draper declares, "was thronged with infidel delegates: some came to discuss philosophical questions, some were bearers of presents. Elephants and a bevy of dancing girls were courteously sent by the sultan to his friend, who, it is said, was not insensible to the witcheries of these Oriental beauties. He wore a Saracen dress. In his privacy he did not hesitate to say, 'I came not here to deliver the Holy City, but to maintain my estimation among the Franks.'"

Indeed, he did more than that. In the Mohammedan atmosphere he frankly explained that the pope could not have done other than excommunicate him, unless he desired to lay himself open to the mockery and revilings of the Christian peoples. In order to show his love for the Sultan of Babylon, he presented him with the consecrated sword he had taken from the altar of St. Peter. No passage of arms occurred in this remarkable expedition; not a drop of blood was spent, not a lance splintered save in courtesy. The sultan was willing the emperor, his good friend, should have Jerusalem, the elephants, the dancing girls—anything his heart might desire; and the Christian champion, not to be outdone in generosity, turned the temple of Solomon over to the Mohammedan custody, and bound himself by oath to resist any attack which might be made upon the sultan by Christian swords. It was a treaty worthy of the enlightened monarch under whose protection, if not from whose hand, the book *Di Tribus Impostoribus* was given to the world.

Meanwhile, Duke Rainaldo, Frederick's loyal vassal, was invading the Papal States, and was checked only by the arms of John of Brienne, one of the vassals of the church. This attack—that of a vassal on his sovereign—led the pope to absolve the subjects of Frederick in Sicily from their allegiance.

After his return to Italy, Frederick found it convenient to be reconciled to the church, and he made promises of reform and restitution at San Germano and visited Gregory at Anagni. His letters at that time are full of his admiration for the amiability and

goodness of the pontiff. But the freebooter instinct
and the spirit of domination were too strong in the
Sicilian; he began to rob the Templars and the Hospitallers who were not among his supporters. The
pope reproached him, and he again sought the latter's
help when his son Henry, who had been crowned king
of Germany, revolted against him. Henry deposed
and in prison, however, he was free once more, and his
Saracens robbed churches while he tyrannized over
Sicily and oppressed the Lombards. Travellers in his
dominions were not safe; they were taken by his Moslem swordsmen, thrown into prison, and held for
ransom. These infidel warriors were allowed free
pillage of a church at Lucera. He had always jeered
at the popes, laughing at the religious ceremonies, and
meriting the reproach of Gregory, "Out of the sea a
beast is risen whose name is written all over, 'Blasphemy.'" In 1239, when he was at the height of his
power, Gregory renewed the excommunication.

Judged by any system of politics the human world
has ever known, what amazing politicians are these of
the church? Never is it the weak and the humble they
strike with the spiritual sword; always the strong and
the proud. A veritable hurricane of fire Gregory in-
voked by his sentence. Frederick rages with his Saracens up and down Italy. He writes to his son that,
despite the fair offers of the pope, he will bring matters to issue with the sword, will humble the high
priest and so treat him that never again will he dare
open his mouth against the emperor. A fugitive from
the infidel warriors of the Christian emperor, the aged
and troubled Gregory dies at last in 1241, and in

coarse jest the enlightened monarch informs Europe
of the fact. Another of the papal politicians of conventional history has obtained his reward: he has
peace.

But still Frederick ravages the Estates of the
Church, still he clings to the cardinals he has taken
prisoners from the highroads of the empire, until the
French king's threats cause him to release those who
were subject to that monarch, and Celestine IV's
short pontificate is followed by the reign of Pope Innocent IV. Innocent endeavored to bring about
peace, but the emperor declared that he must have
forgiveness of his sins before he would show proof of
repentance, that he would hold his ecclesiastical cap-
tives until he received absolution. So Innocent was
compelled to give up hope and to flee from Rome and
into France; and there, at the Council of Lyons, Frederick was tried on charges of heresy, sacrilege, immorality, perjury, and blasphemy. The anathema of
the church was hurled at him by those fugitive but
fearless priests. They inverted the torches, quenched
the burning flax. "So may he be extinguished!" they
said. And after recounting his deeds, Draper says,
"Forsaken and alone, he died."

CHAPTER VI

TWO FRENCH PHILIPS

THE law of nations that gave the pope the right to protect the person and property of a crusader in the kingdom of any Christian prince whatsoever was thoroughly understood by the princes of the middle ages, and none made protest against it, although some violated it. It grew out of the necessities of the time. If there was to be any united action of Christian warriors against the infidel —and political wisdom no less than religious zeal pointed out the desirability of such Christian concert —some warder there must be to protect the holdings of the absent lord. They didn't trust their neighbors much in that freebooter age. They did trust the pope. Knightly honor was a fine, high-sounding thing, but papal justice was considered a safer dependence. Thus the papacy became the great court of equity of Christendom, to which the injured turned naturally and promptly for redress. Its competence was never questioned then, although its decrees might be evaded and at times disobeyed.

It was by no means a light or a safe function to exercise, this of bending to justice the proud and unbridled monarchs of young Europe. The naked hand that was stretched forth to take the loot from the iron-gloved fist of a robber prince, took the chance of being crushed. The priest, who wore but the frail vestments of his office, ran the risk of being bruised among the jostling warriors in their harness of steel. Yet the courage of that great court seems to have sustained it always. Time and again popes rushed on what seemed like certain destruction, leaving the issue to God. The annals are full of their expressions of human despair not for themselves, but for the church, and yet there must have been underneath that despair a faith in their cause that was sublime; for in the face of the calamities their human vision foresaw, they pressed on to the end in the course they had adopted.

If it was priestcraft, it was a craft such as no priesthood elsewhere has ever exhibited. If it was political wisdom, it transcended the wisdom of human politicians.

It was from the exercise of his judicial function in the case of Richard of England that Pope Celestine turned to admonish the powerful warrior Philip Augustus, crusader and Christian king of France. A man just humanly wise would not have sought this additional trouble, for Celestine had difficulties enough. Richard—that same Richard who is the idol of English chivalry, the Lion-heart of romance—was taken a prisoner on his way home from Palestine by Leopold, duke of Austria, who held him for ransom. Henry, the German emperor, was implicated in this bit of brigandage, and the wife of Richard appealed to the pope against both of them. Immediately the pope demanded from the duke and the emperor the release of the royal crusader. Leopold insisted on his ransom, and was excommunicated. Richard, free now, appealed to the pope to have the money restored to him, and the pope again summoned to the bar of justice the great emperor.

While this controversy was on, and the pope was deep in the work of enforcing justice, Philip Augustus of France fell in love with a beautiful girl who is known in history as Agnes of Meran. There was an obstacle in the path of his heart's desire: he had a living wife. Some time before he had married the sister of King Canute II of Denmark, Ingeburge, a fair, high-spirited, and virtuous princess. Ingeburge was the fifth cousin of Isabella, the first wife of Philip, and this relationship served for a pretext upon which a synod of political bishops granted the king a divorce. Ingeburge's angry protest resulted in her imprisonment, and she laid her complaint before the pope through the ambassadors of her brother, the Danish monarch.

Celestine, as a preliminary, set aside the decree of the Synod of Compiègne and sent his own legates to France to examine into the merits of the king's case. At the same time he warned Philip against marrying again, but his admonition the king disregarded; his nuptials with the fair Agnes were solemnized, and Ingeburge was imprisoned and treated with greater harshness than before.

Celestine died, and Innocent III ascended to the throne of the popes. In its order there came before Innocent this case of the King of France, and in September of the year 1198 the pope sent a letter to the king by the hand of Cardinal Petrus. In this letter the pope protests the reluctance with which he takes any action against France, but declares that his stern duty obliges him to take all means to turn Philip from the path of sin, particularly as his example is encouraging lesser princes to break their marriage vows. Philip remained obdurate, and Petrus, in pursuance of his commission, convoked the Council of Dijon, where was discussed the interdict under which it was proposed to lay France. The king appeared before the council and pleaded for time for reflection, and it was granted to him. But Philip could not bear the separation from Agnes, and at length Petrus summoned the Council of Vienne and pronounced the interdict, in the name of the pope, on January 14, 1200.

The anger of the king was raging. He cursed the pope; he declared he would become a Mohammedan; he banished the bishops who had attended the council, and laid a heavy hand on the priests in whose silent churches no mass was said.

But the pope remained firm; the land lay under the interdict; the priests of the church gave no sacrament; and the king's anger gave place to distress. He assured the pope of his submission, and Innocent sent a kinsman of the monarch to France to lift the interdict. The churches were opened, the mass was celebrated, all the functions of religion were again exercised, to the great joy of the people. For seven months the pall had rested on France.

The pope made arrangements for the Synod of Soissons, and bade Ingeburge and her brother forward their witnesses. The council convened, and the case came for trial before it. But Philip anticipated the verdict; he admitted the claim of Ingeburge, and promised to restore her to her proper place as queen.

He complained bitterly to Pope Innocent, however, and this was Innocent's reply: that he could not deviate from the right path and offend the Heavenly King for the sake of an earthly one. Still Philip sought for a long period to have the divorce case reopened; even after the death of Agnes he could not forgive her rival. The pope did declare the two children of Agnes legitimate, on the ground that she had married Philip in good faith after the publication of the decree of the Synod of Compiègne; but in 1212 he wrote to Philip saying that the divorce the monarch sought could not be granted, and urging the king to cease his importunities. Philip then took Ingeburge into his palace, and his will, which was published after his death, is full of praise of her virtue and devotion.

This is an incident in history which Professor Draper calls an interference with the civil affairs of France upon the "pretext" of composing a matrimonial difficulty. Before passing on from this to the greater struggle of a century later, from Philip the Great to Philip the Fair, let us give sufficient consideration to one phase of it. *When the king wanted his marriage annulled, he appealed to the ecclesiastical court.* It was Philip who brought the matter before the church; it was Philip who assembled the Synod of Compiègne; the initiative was all with Philip. If he was angered at the determination of the judge, he was no more than has been many another unsuccessful litigant.

I always think the story of the great battle between Philip the Fair and Pope Boniface VIII should be read backward: that the conduct of the king cannot be

well understood if we do not at the outset enlighten
our understanding with what followed the death of
Boniface. The reader of history will recall that within
a year of the death of this pope a French pope ascended the throne of St. Peter and transferred his
residence from Rome to Avignon in France, and that
for seventy years thereafter Avignon was the seat of
the papacy. It is a period known in the history of the
church as the "Seventy Years' Captivity." A passion
for a fair face and an imperious impatience of check
and bridle are at the base of the controversy of Philip
Augustus with the church, but it is a different matter
with Philip the Fair. Policy moves him; a cold and
calculating political design, shrewdly composed by
crafty lawyers, holds his course to its prescription
throughout. At the end of that design was the subjugation of the papacy, its administration under
French influence and for the benefit of the French
monarch. It was a lawyers' battle, for if Flotte and
de Nogaret, the king's advisers, were bold and skilful, their opponent was himself a master jurist. Bene-
detto Gaetani, who became Pope Boniface VIII, had
been educated in the famous University of Paris, and
had mastered canon law at Bologna. Prior to his
elevation to the supreme office he had been an active
servant of the church in many lands. He had visited
England and Germany, and in 1290, when Philip the
Fair was a young man, Cardinal Gaetani was papal
legate in France. In July, 1294, Celestine V was
elected pope. He was a pious hermit, eighty years
old, and he soon found that the burdens of the high
office were beyond his strength. In December he

voluntarily took the heavy triple crown from his own brows and laid it down. His abdication was followed by the election of Cardinal Gaetani. It was upon this point that the lawyers of Philip's court were to seize later.

Boniface had the same great ambition that had animated his predecessors: he hoped fervently for a successful crusade. To that end he shaped all his efforts: he busied himself in preparation; he planned the organization of a mighty Christian host; he gathered gold for the war-chest of the faithful. As this subject of the collection of treasure furnishes one of the points of dispute with Philip, and as the impression one gets from conventional history is that the greed of the papacy drained Europe of its wealth, it is well to devote a thought to it. To read the common histories is to acquire the belief that every pope desired to enrich himself and his relatives, and to that end he laid heavy taxes on all the Christian world. It is only by accident that the thought of another use for all the funds accumulated by the church may be stirred by reading of the beggar relieved at the monastery gate, of the great hospitals erected for the relief of the poor and the afflicted, of the schools and institutions of learning, of the mighty efforts put forth for the reclamation of the Holy Land. Ranke gives shape to the thought when he is discussing papal finances in the fifteenth century.

"There has doubtless been justice," he says, "in the complaints raised against the exactions of Rome during the fifteenth century; but it is true also that of the proceeds a small part only passed into the hands of the popes. Pius II enjoyed the obedience of all Europe, yet he once suffered so extreme a dearth of money that he was forced to restrict himself and his household to one meal a day."

Boniface found the political condition of Europe anything but favorable to his plans with regard to the East. There was war everywhere; the greed and jealousy of the Christian monarchs filled the whole land with outrage and battle. The Estates of the Church were used by the monarchs to furnish their war-chests, and, following the example of their sovereigns, the nobility entered with enthusiasm into the congenial labor of pillaging churches and monasteries. The ambition of Philip the Fair alarmed Edward I of England and King Adolphus of Germany, who joined their forces and did battle against France. It was to compose these difficulties that the pope addressed himself, and he had an obvious and legitimate object in view—the pacification of Christendom and the proposed war on the infidels. He succeeded at last in persuading the Englishman and the German to accept his mediation, but while negotiations were in progress Philip again set the torch to the thatch by violently taking prisoners the Count of Flanders and his wife and daughter, the last named the betrothed of the English king. At the same time he made an alliance with the Scottish monarch and again assailed England.

Meanwhile from all the war-swept lands, but particularly from France, arose the complaints of the ecclesiastical authorities with regard to the heavy tax laid upon them by the kings. In France the raising of funds from the churches had been turned over to royal officers, who did not neglect the opportunity of lining their own pockets with the spoil of the church. These complaints reached Boniface about the same time that the Count of Flanders appealed to him against the forcible detention of his daughter in the hands of the French king. Boniface sent the Bishop of Mieux to investigate, and then, after a consultation with the cardinals, issued the bull known as *Clericis laicos*. That was in 1296, and the bull prohibited, on pain of excommunication, the taxation of ecclesiastical property without the consent of the pope. If such a prohibition strikes us as odd, we should remember that we live in the twentieth century, and that this was in the thirteenth; that the recognized common law is not now what it then was; and even to-day no nation taxes the property of another nation.

Philip did not question the legality of that bull, but he took measures of reprisal. He uttered a decree forbidding foreigners to engage in commerce in France and prohibiting the exportation of treasure. This prohibition was a blow at the donations for the crusades.

The bull *Ineffabilis*, which the pope sent to Philip on September 25, 1296, declared that his former pronouncement was but the crystallization of well-recognized canon law, designed to prevent the abuse of power by the royal officers and not to affect bona-fide contributions to the royal treasury. Neither did it affect any tribute due under the feudal obligation. The pope declared it was far from his intention to cripple the government, that he would rather have the clergy sell the jewels from the altars than expose the kingdom to danger; but, on the other hand—and here is expressed the strange expectation of these politicians of the church—he was ready to suffer persecution, exile, and death for the liberty of the church. That was what they looked forward to when they raised up the Cross before the eyes of powerful princes: not the altitude of power and latitude of dominion with which human statesmanship concerns itself, but *persecution* and *exile* and *death.*

Philip had gained victories in the field, and for a time he assumed a more peaceful attitude toward the pope. He sent a deputation to Rome, and the pope modified his bull so as to exempt from the taxation prohibition cases of necessity, the king to judge of the necessity. On his side, the king revoked his orders prohibiting the exportation of jewels and precious metals. The canonization of Louis IX, the grandfather of Philip, occurring at this time, added to the good feeling between France and Rome. This happy condition lasted until Boniface was called upon to arbitrate between France and England. The decision of the arbitrator did not please Philip; and although the French king submitted, he and his nobles began to enrich themselves at the expense of the churches. Philip seized the estate of the Bishop of Maguelonne, and took over for the royal treasury the funds bequeathed by Cardinal John of St. Cecilia to the charities. Other nobles made free with church property whenever convenient: Count Robert took with the sword the town of the Bishop of Cambray. Meanwhile the French court was a refuge for the rebellious Colonnas, who vented their spite against Boniface in the most amazing aspersions of his character and conduct.

It was to this court that Boniface sent Bernard de Saisset, Bishop of Pamiers, early in 1301, with a plea to Philip to allow the church tithes to be used for the great crusade. A rude reception the papal nuncio found in France. He was made a prisoner, despoiled of his property, and his servants were cast into cells and put to the torture in order to extract from them confessions upon which Peter Flotte might base a charge of conspiracy against the throne. Before a court assembled by Philip the bishop was haled, Flotte confronting him with his accusation of high treason and the depositions of the servants on the rack. The papal nuncio contented himself with a denial of the competency of the court, and he was convicted and placed in the custody of the Archbishop of Narbonne.

This was bitter news for the aged pontiff, beset on one side by the German monarch and threatened now with the vengeance of an angry French king. On December 5, 1301, he prepared a bull demanding the possessions and the person of his messenger from Philip. This was the famous bull that the critics of the papacy have held up as a shining example of the arrogance and far-reaching temporal aggressiveness of the church. It takes its title from its opening words, *"Ausculta, fili carissimi."* "Listen, dearest son," the aged pope says to the king, to whose notice he then brings all the ills the church has suffered: the attacks upon travellers on their way to and from

Rome; the oppression of the church of Lyons, which was not in the kingdom of France: all the sins of the monarch, among them the debasement of the coinage which had caused so much suffering among his subjects. "God has set us, however unworthy, over kings and kingdoms," he said.

Philip had his spies in the consistory, and they brought advance information of the nature and phraseology of the bull. The words quoted above made their suggestion to the political instinct of Peter Flotte, and the scene was set for the great coup of Philip when Jacques de Norman arrived at court with the pope's message. Philip had granted audience to Jacques, who was Archbishop of Narbonne, and, seated on his throne in his great hall, with his fiery nobles around him, he awaited the stately prelate, who advanced with the document in his hand. Suddenly from the circle of courtiers sprang forth the Count of Artois, cousin of Philip and famed as a freebooter throughout the realm of France. With a rude hand he tore from the astonished archbishop the great roll and flung it among the blazing logs in the chimney-place. De Norman's angry protest was still in the air when the count placed in the king's hand the document known in history as "the short document." Flotte had made good use of the advance information; the paper the king now held contained some of the expressions of the original bull, but its principal declaration was that God had set the pope above the king in matters spiritual *and temporal.* The archbishop's denunciation of the forgery, his indignant declaration that the bull had contained nothing with regard to temporal matters, went unheeded; throughout the kingdom was published "the short document" and the king's letter in reply, a letter whose style was suspiciously similar to that of the counterfeited bull.

By every means that clever politicians could contrive the patriotism of France was inflamed, the cry of "papal aggression" rang from one end to the other of Philip's wide dominions. The people were told that the nation was in danger, that the Italians were to rule them by order of the pope. Not only that, but by order of a false pope, a pope illegally elected and not entitled to supremacy even in ecclesiastical matters.

Philip proclaimed himself the leader of the national movement; the defender of France against Italian aggression. On April 10, 1302, he assembled the Parliament of the Three Estates, before whom Flotte made an eloquent and impassioned speech, denouncing the papal aggression in temporal matters. Philip appealed to the delegates to stand by him "as their friend and as their king." The robber nobles, to whom the pillage of church property was a most attractive prospect, in a very hysteria of loyalty resolved to stand by the king; and the popular deputies, overawed by the fierce warriors of the superior order, and led by all the wild clamor to believe that the squadrons of the pope were already riding over the borders of France, did not demur. The clergy asked time to deliberate, but the nobles and political agents went among them with threats, and they at last signed the letters the king desired. Even then, it was "with bitter tears," as they said, that they addressed their remonstrance to the pope, refusing to obey his summons to a council in Rome because they had been forbidden by the king to go to the Eternal City. The bull *Ausculta fili* had commanded the clergy to attend the council in Rome in order that they might there discuss the matters in controversy between their pope and their king.

Philip could now boast that all France was behind him in his opposition to Boniface. The nobles had addressed a letter to the cardinals, complaining of the pope, and intimating that they would undertake a general crusade should the College of Cardinals "bring matters to a termination" in accordance with the king's desire. The cardinals replied with indignation that the bull had been discussed in consistory and approved by them, and that it contained no such temporal pretensions as those against which complaint was made. Boniface's answer to the bishops contains a similar denial; he accuses Flotte of originating the intrigue, as he terms it.

Pressing now his assault upon Boniface, Philip sent his envoys and some of his clergy to a consistory held in August, 1302, over which the Cardinal Bishop of Porte presided. That dignitary gave little comfort to the French king's representatives. In his speech to the consistory he denied the authenticity of "the short document."

"If prelates are called to Rome to deliberate," he said, turning upon the French envoys, "it is not the opponents of the king, but his special confidants, who are summoned; and not to the end of the world, but to Rome."

There was found in the Church of St. Victor in Paris a codex of the address of Boniface, and although it is doubtful if it truly represents what the pope said, it probably contains much of his speech. Boniface bitterly attacked Flotte, the Count of Artois, and the Count of St. Pol. Flotte, he declared, had falsified his bull by representing the pope as having declared that the king must hold France as a fief from him.

"It is forty years," the pontiff protests, "since we mastered jurisprudence, and we know that God ordains there shall be two powers: who, then, can or dare believe that such a foolish sentiment came from us? We declare that we do not desire to trespass on the king's jurisdiction in anything. But neither the king nor any other Christian can deny that *in matters of sin* he is subject to us."

He has not only not sought to deprive the king of any prerogative, but, in so far as it was lawful for him to do so, he has forborne to interfere in ecclesiastical affairs within the kingdom. He consented to the appointment of the prebends to the Church of Paris by the king, stipulating only that the appointees be "masters of theology, or doctors of law, or other learned persons, and not nephews and relations of this and that person"; but the king had appointed only "worthless favorites."

"Let the cardinals decide between us," the pontiff proposed. "Send some upright nobles to Rome—the Duke of Burgundy or the Count of Brittany, or such like—who can tell me in what I have erred and whom I have troubled."

But Philip had no intention of trusting his cause to a tribunal not under his own thumb. His agents continue to clamor in France against the Italian aggression, his nobles oppress such ecclesiastics as are faithful to the church, and the roads are not safe for pilgrims on their way to Rome. In that city in October, 1302, Boniface promulgates at the great synod two bulls. The first pronounces excommunication against any one, of whatever degree, who molests travellers to or from the seat of the Holy See. The second was the celebrated bull *Unam sanctam,* which was an argument of the principle of the power of popes to judge princes in the administration of their states *in so far as the church was affected thereby.* It was simply a statement of the canon and the public law of Europe at that time, and the principle it stated was by no means that *states* were subject to the church, but that *princes* no less than subjects were accountable for their conduct to God. As the pope was the vicar of Christ, it followed that every human being was subject to the pope. As there can be no question as to the ability of Boniface as a lawyer, it may be taken for granted that what he stated was good law at that time. It was absolutely conclusive against those who admitted his major premise that the pope was the vicar of God, and not Philip or one of his advisers ever held to the contrary. The modern who reads it must keep in mind the personal character of government in that day, and the distinction between *states* and *princes in the administration of their states,* which is by no means a hair-fine distinction. Can there be any doubt that the public officer of to-day, mayor or governor or president, who is dishonest, or oppressive, or unjust *in the administration of his office,* violates the precepts of his religion, Catholic or Protestant, and is individually responsible to God? Does any church claiming divine authority hold less to-day in this regard than did Boniface VIII in the much misrepresented bull *Unam sanctam?*

Death deprived Philip of two of his boldest supporters. His cousin, the Count of Artois, and Peter Flotte were gone, but at his side was a counsellor less skilful but more malignant than Flotte had been. William de Nogaret, keeper of the seals and friend of the Colonnas, became all-powerful at the French court. Philip had made an answer to the pope's complaint in which he had laid the blame for some of his actions upon the shoulders of officers who had exceeded their authority, and had calmly ignored other causes of complaint. He made a vague and general promise of reform, but the pope could see in it no real intention of a change of policy.

In March, 1303, another of the spectacular incidents of the controversy interested the court. De Nogaret publicly challenged the king to protect Holy Church against Boniface, "the interloper, false pope, thief, robber, heretic, simonist," and to convoke a general council for his deposition. Philip assembled thirty of his political prelates, who heard on June 13, 1303, the charges that had been prepared. The Lord of Vezenobre, du Plessis, opened the attack. He laid at the door of Boniface every abomination the fertile mind of the day could imagine. He appealed to Philip to insist upon a general council for the trial of so great a criminal. Other nobles followed in the same strain, and then Philip promised that he would try to have a general council convened. He appealed, he said, to the future general council and the future true·pope.

A petition, drawn in the spirit of this convention, was circulated for signature. The king's servants had some difficulty in getting it signed. The Abbot of Citeaux was thrown into prison for refusing to write his name to it. The Abbots of Cluny and Prémontré also suffered incarceration for the same cause, and the Dominican monks of Montpellier were driven out of the kingdom because they refused to lend their names to Philip's accusations. The king undertook to justify himself in the face of the world by letters he sent to the princes of Europe.

Meanwhile Boniface held a consistory at Anagni, and in the presence of the cardinals solemnly swore that the charges against him were false. He took over the French benefices and announced the preparation of the bull of excommunication against Philip. For, contrary to the impression one gets from conventional history, Philip had not been excommunicated by name. As one of those who had molested travellers and despoiled church property, he had fallen under the ban pronounced against such offenders in general, but he had not been pointed out by the voice of the church as one cut off and accursed.

This the court resolved to prevent, by violence if necessary. The Colonnas were kept well advised by their spies of what was passing in Anagni, and de Nogaret and Sciarra Colonna, with a huge treasure-chest, hurried into Italy. They gathered together some rebellious lords of the Papal States, and hired a band of those banditti whose swords were always on the market for any purpose whatever. With a force of these formidable free companions at his back, de Nogaret appeared before the walls of Anagni on September 7, 1303. Treachery opened the gates to him, and his mercenaries poured into the town. The papal guard was beaten back; the household of the pope fled. De Nogaret's followers pillaged the palace, destroying the archives and thus blotting out documents which might have thrown much light upon this controversy.

The wild uproar in the palace apprised Boniface that his enemies were under his roof, but there was no fear in the heart of the aged pontiff. "Open the doors of my apartments," he imperiously ordered those who still gathered around him, "for I will suffer martyrdom for the church of God! As I am taken, like Christ, by treachery, I will die as pope!"

He clothed his body with the majestic vestments of his office; he set upon his own brow, wrinkled with thought and trouble, the towering triple crown. Proudly straightening the back that eighty-six years had bowed down, he ascended the throne of Peter, and there he sat with calm eyes regarding the crowd of men in steel coats and with bloody swords who streamed into his audience-chamber. By his side were two of the princes of the church who had remained with him, the Cardinals Nicholas Boccasin and Peter d'Espagne. Before that splendid and venerable figure the rude soldiers shrank back, and, with eyes that never faltered, Boniface saw de Nogaret and Sciarra Colonna push to the front, a naked blade in the hand of the Italian. Colonna leaped up the step and drew back his mailed fist to strike, but de Nogaret pulled down his arm. The servant of the French king had insults to heap upon this old man whose tranquil eyes regarded him with so deep a pity. From his breast he drew the accusation of the Assembly of Paris, and in a loud tone he read it. Finding the pope still silent when he had concluded, his anger surged up to his brain and he cried out:

"I will have you taken to Lyons in chains to be tried by a general council and deposed!"

Then for the first time Boniface spoke.

"Here is my head and here is my neck!" he answered in the rich, firm voice that had made him noted among the preachers of the church. "For the liberty of the church I will submit, as Catholic, as lawful pope, and as vicar of Jesus Christ, to be condemned by the *paterini;* for I desire martyrdom for faith in Christ and his church!"

The rage of de Nogaret blazed out in an imprecation, and he grasped the pontiff and tore him from his seat. As Boniface staggered at the foot of his throne, Colonna struck him. Cries of "Malefactor!" "Cursed malefactor!" rose from the soldiers, who, steeled as they were against pity, were horrified at the violence offered to the venerable head of the faith. But Colonna and de Nogaret sternly silenced the malcontents and drove the pope to the castle of a noble in the town, who had sought his own advantage by entering into a league with the French. There an attempt was made to starve the pope into an agreement to abdicate, but neither blows nor privation could shake the spirit of that old man. He bore his ordeal with weakening bodily but unimpaired spiritual strength.

De Nogaret had hoped to return to France with the pope's abdication, but he was doomed to disappointment. The horrified townspeople, who had been awed by the military strength of de Nogaret's following, began to murmur, and the sense of outrage emboldened them. There were little assemblages in the smithy, in the shop of the barber, in front of the doors of the substantial citizens; the tradesmen in the market-place glowered at the swaggering free companions in their iron headpieces. It needed but a leader to gather these together, and the leader was found in Cardinal del Fiesco. Three days after the attack upon Boniface the cry of "Long live the pope! Death to the traitors!" resounded in the quiet streets of Anagni, and de Nogaret and his band found themselves furiously assailed by a mob of townspeople headed by the cardinal. Despite their discipline, they were driven outside the walls. The pope was released. He called a consistory at once, and his first words were a proclamation of pardon to those who had subjected him to so much pain and indignity.

Meanwhile the Colonnas had gathered partisans and were besieging Anagni. The news of the attack spread over the country, and in Rome the Orsini, hereditary enemies of the Colonnas, prepared to take partisan advantage of the situation. Gathering their men-at-arms, they rode with all speed to Anagni and relieved the town. They brought Boniface back with them to Rome. But the privations to which he had been subjected were too much for the frame of so old a man: thirty-five days only he survived the outrage of Anagni.

Benedict XI reigned only six months, but it was sufficient for him to express his horror over the attack upon the person of his predecessor. There followed him in the papal chair Clement V, the first of a long succession of French popes. Philip now believed he had won the long fight; henceforth the popes were to dwell at Avignon. But hatred of the pontiff who had so long defied him, or perhaps a desire for the vindication in the eyes of the world which the condemnation of that pope's memory might give him, urged him to importune Clement to call a council for the trial of the old charges. At last Clement yielded so far that he convened the general council. But there the artificiality of Philip's case became so apparent, and so many of the learned and saintly fathers of the church came forward to defend Boniface's memory, that the French politicians considered it expedient to divert public attention by sensational charges made against the Knights Templars. The pope insisted on some disposition of the case of Boniface, although Philip desired simply to have it dropped. Finally, however, there appeared before the council three knights in armor, and before the bar of that ecclesiastical court they threw down their gauntlets, while the herald proclaimed their readiness to defend with their bodies the holiness of life of Boniface. None appeared to gainsay them. Thus they settled the case according to the custom of those days.

CHAPTER VII

THE GHOST OF A SPANISH KING

THREE citizens of the American Republic have just been elevated by ordination of Pope Pius X to a rank that had its origin in the Roman catacombs. They have entered the senate of their church, which was organized under the direction of that Hildebrand who afterward became Pope Gregory VII. Having left the modern cities of Boston and New York—the Boston and New York we know, that are alive with the fullness of the spirit of this age; having crossed the Atlantic in great vessels propelled by steam-power; having flashed messages to friends from mid-ocean by means of a modern miracle, the wireless telegraph; having traversed that ancient Gaul, in which St. Boniface preached, in cars drawn by steam-locomotives; having ridden in automobiles through the streets of the city of the Cæsars, they kneel before the altar of the great Church of St. Peter, whose foundations were laid, four decades before Columbus sailed from Palos, upon the last resting-place of that Peter who was Prince of the Apostles of Jesus Christ!

Incidents such as this *realize* history for us; they are the living, tangible bonds between us and the distant past; they connect the things which are familiar, visible, intimate, with the things that are strange,

ghostly, and remote; they are to a doubting generation as were the wounds of the Saviour which the
doubting Thomas must touch with his own hands.

They help us to invest with flesh and blood and vi-
talize with spirit the figures that history presents to us.
They make it easier for us to form a mental picture of
the Julius II with whom Michelangelo talked of this
very dome beneath which Pius X and the American
cardinals kneel to-day. We see the flashing eyes of the
master sculptor as he urges his mighty project upon
the pope: "Think, your Holiness, of this vast dome,
this replica of the ancient Roman Pantheon, elevated
upon great columns to typify the elevation of our holy
faith over that paganism which once found its home in
the Pantheon; think of so majestic a structure in
which all that is noble and beautiful shall find expression, its base comprehending the world beneath it, its
foundations on the grave of the martyred Peter, and
its apex lifted high in glorification of the Son of God!"
We can better understand the enthusiasm of the great
soldier-pope, the impatience with which he had torn
down the ancient basilica in order that so vast a project should not be hampered for lack of room; the opposition of some of the cardinals who represented the
love the medieval world had for the old church with
all its great memories. These things come nearer to
us; they are clearer to our sight because of the ceremonies whereby Cardinals Farley, Falconio, and
O'Connell have just been inducted into the senate of
their ancient church.

Julius II came to the throne of Peter when the warlike spirit of Europe was changing in its character. It

was more fierce and cruel than ever it had been, but it was no longer devotional. The church still cherished the design of reclaiming the Holy Land, but the princes were interested in nothing but territorial extension and political power. The old fluid condition of European politics was passing away; states were solidifying, national boundaries growing more definite. No man can play a great part in any age without being influenced by the spirit of that age, and Julius II, when he received the Ring of the Fisherman, had a great part to play. The personal immorality of Alexander VI, the cruelty and rapacity of Cæsar Borgia, had not only weakened the moral prestige of the papacy, but had ruined the Papal States. Everywhere there was rebellion, everywhere in the domain of the church there was lack of respect for law. Free companions plundered the cities, and nobles and their henchmen robbed and murdered on the public roads. Proud vassals laughed at the enfeebled papacy, and tyrannized over the common people. The north of Italy had been lost to the States of the Church, the German power shadowed all Italy.

Without a clear understanding of all this, and of the thoughts and motives of the princes of Europe, we cannot understand how political conditions influenced the thought and literature of the Reformation and the attitude of Protestant peoples toward the church from which they had separated. It was never the theological consideration that embittered Catholic against Protestant and Protestant against Catholic; it was ever the breath of secular politics that fanned the flame of hatred and blackened history for three centuries with the most remarkable falsehoods. A division on points of doctrine there might have been, otherwise; but it would never have left us with prejudices so blind that our every thought of the commonest problems must be made insane by the hatred we have for fellow-Christians.

We do not have to go in this day to Catholic historians for proof that this is so. A reading of our own accepted historians shows it so clearly that it is strange that every one who reads them does not see it instantly. The Great Schism was due to the interference of the temporal rulers with ecclesiastical affairs. That interference left a Catholic world with two claimants to the papacy, and a wide-spread doubt as to which had the right on his side. It was settled at the Council of Constance, but in the meantime it had been made the tool of politics. By confusing the people it had allowed the princes to shift from side to side, as suited them, without fear of such consequences as would follow in the days when, despite the election of antipopes, there was no doubt among the people as to the identity of the true pope. Ranke points this out. "It was long at the option of each prince," he says, "to attach himself to one pope or the other, *as might best suit his political interests.*"

And the princes were only seeking some such pretext. Remember, it was the day of personal government, of absolutism in politics, the day when the favor or disfavor of a prince meant life or death to a subject! The "civil power," of which we hear so much, didn't mean a "government of the people, by the people, for the people"; it meant a Henry, or a Conrad, or a

Philip, or a Louis, who might happen to be born a
king. They were robbing one another whenever opportunity offered, and the people all the time; they
were indulging every passion without scruple and
without check—"the king could do no wrong."
Where was the bar at which he could be arraigned,
where was the judge to try him? There was only one
such to pass upon his moral guilt, and he went as far
as he dared to defy and oppress that. No wonder that,
as the Protestant historian we have quoted says, "The
civil power would no longer endure the presence of
any higher authority." No wonder that the popes
themselves looked to the material sword to protect
them against so conscienceless a band of tyrants as
then cursed Europe.

"I had once thought," exclaimed a speaker at the
Council of Basel, "that the secular power should be
wholly separate from that of the church; but I have
now learned that virtue without force is but slightly
respected, and that the pope, without the patrimony
of the church, would be the mere servant of kings and
princes!"

Indeed, the princes had done much toward impair-
ing the moral value of the church. They had made
the great bishoprics crown patronage; it was a poor
monarch who did not have a vassal prelate riding in
mail among his men-at-arms, and a profligate archbishop of his own appointment making jest of holy
things at his court, while a hired substitute performed
his pastoral duties.

Into such a world came Pope Julius II to talk to
such princes in the only language for which they had

any respect. He was not a young man when he ascended the chair of St. Peter and received the temporal crown of the Papal States with the spiritual crown of the Bishop of Rome, but he undertook the warfare for the pacification and reclamation of the patrimony of the church with the zeal and strength and skill of a spirit upon which the passing years seemed to have no effect. The boasting nobles of Italy first felt his power; he cleared the roads of robbers, peasant and noble alike. The bandit business became unprofitable and extremely dangerous. Everywhere in the tyrant-ridden States of the Church the armed priest appeared as a liberator, and the people thereafter rejoiced in just and benignant government. It was by the sword that Julius regained many of the alienated provinces of the papacy, but it was by bonds of affectionate loyalty that he bound them into a political unit which secular princes learned to dread. He had begun his career of conquest by calling the Swiss to his aid; he needed no foreign soldiery when once the people learned of the beneficence and justice of his government. "Time was," Machiavelli writes, "when no baron was so insignificant but that he might venture to brave the papal power: now it is regarded with respect even by a king of France."

But he not only consolidated and strengthened the Papal States, and reclaimed from the Venetians those cities they had seized: he freed all Italy from the shadow of foreign domination. Before the sword of this soldier-priest, who in his old age would lead his knights across the bloody field and into the breach of a battered wall, the German invaders were driven into their own boundaries and the German power was humiliated by the loss of northern Italy.

The consequences of this were tremendous. The national pride of Germany had been hurt by a pope; one of the despised Latin race had broken the warlike Teuton's power. All the bitterness of a war between races found expression in calumnies of the pope and the Italians. It was reported throughout Germany that Rome was full of evil things, that the papacy was being used to humiliate and dismember the empire.

To me it seems that Julius II would have had the praise of the world had he been but one of the two things he was. He was splendid as a patriot; as a soldier he had no superior among the generals of the day; as a prince he was just and wise. On the other hand, his devotion was pure and his piety profound, his mind was enlightened, and the budding flower of the Renaissance which was to burst into full bloom in the reign of Leo X was sympathetically nurtured by Julius. As a pope he was admirable; as a prince he was admirable: but as pope and prince, he sowed political prejudice deep in the breast of Germany.

Less than ever after the day of Julius were the princes of Europe disposed to bear the check of the papal influence. He had planted in their mind the suggestion that a pope might arise with the spirit of a Cæsar and the temper of a Julius, with a vast project of consolidating politically a great Christian state, and little did they relish such a notion. "It was now the time," says Ranke, "when the European kingdoms were finally consolidating their forces after long struggles. The papacy, interfering in all things and seeking to dominate all, came very soon to be re-garded *in a political point of view;* the temporal princes now began to put forth higher claims than they had done hitherto."

But it was not only that their spirit of licentious-ness was chafed: another consideration was making itself felt. Kings and nobles fought, monks worked. The result is simple in economics. The long wars had impoverished the princes; there was not much profit now even in robbing one another, and the wealthy cities had strong walls and paid soldiers to make their despoliation difficult and dangerous. On the other hand, the church properties were rich and unpro-tected. The "thirsting eye of enterprise" rested long-ingly on them. During the fifteenth and sixteenth centuries there were many instances of the appropria-tion of the funds and property of religious by the secular powers. Sometimes it was done under the color of royal proclamation, sometimes it was simple pillage. Sometimes it was accomplished through the agency of political bishops.

The political control of ecclesiastical appointments, against which Gregory VII had fought, had had its effect. The clergy were in a great measure demoral-ized. The court favorites who held the great church benefices by imposition of the kings lived dissolute lives, and the lower clergy in quite considerable num-ber followed the bad example of their superiors. The moral relaxation invaded monasteries, and there is on record a report of that Cardinal Caraffa, who was afterward Pope Paul IV, to Pope Clement, who had sent him to visit the monasteries, in which the cardinal indignantly describes the evil state to which politics had reduced children of the church.

How strange in ears that have heard so much of papal exactions are the words of Ranke, occurring time and again, with regard to the part thereof that really went to the church!

"Participation in ecclesiastical revenues and the right of promotion to church benefices and offices was that which the civil power more especially desired," is one of his illuminating phrases. And he gives us instances. In Spain, King Emanuel calmly takes to himself one-tenth of the property of the church. Henry VII of England assumed the right of nominating bishops, and "appropriated" one-half of the "first fruits" (church tithes). And as to Henry VIII, thus was he "defending the faith," as Ranke tells it: "Before Protestantism had even been thought of by the English sovereign, he had already proceeded to a merciless confiscation of the numerous monasteries." Truly, it was the open season for monasteries.

But now we come to a passage of the greatest significance, because it treats of a period and a place and a project within the youth, the vicinity, and the purview of the great leader of the Reformation.

"In 1500," Ranke says, "the [German] imperial government accorded *one-third only of the sums produced by indulgences to the papal legates, appropriating the remaining two-thirds.*"

Here may we well pause, for it was the charge of the sale of indulgences that more than anything else contributed to the popular success of the Reformation. Princes had their own reasons, doctrinal points might interest the controversial humanists, but to the peasantry of Europe "justification by faith" meant nothing: such subtleties were not for them. The thing that hurt the Catholic Church was the charge that her priests were selling the mercy of God for gold. Melanchthon and his confrères might learnedly draft a confession of faith, but it was Luther who knew how to catch the popular ear and stir the popular indignation.

What, then, is an indulgence?

"An indulgence," says the Rev. Charles Coppens, a Jesuit, "is a remission of the temporal punishment due to sin after the guilt has been remitted. That such punishment may remain after the pardon of a sin, is taught clearly in Holy Scripture, where we read that Nathan said to David: 'The Lord hath taken away thy sin: nevertheless, the child that is born of thee shall die' (2 Kings xiii, 13, 14). Now Christ commissions St. Peter, saying, 'Whatsoever thou shalt loose on earth, it shall be loosed also in heaven' (Matt. xvi, 19). Hence the popes, as successors of St. Peter, claim the power of granting the remission of whatever can keep us out of heaven; both the guilt, by absolution, and the penalty of sin, by indulgences: provided all be done so as to promote the glory of God and the good of souls."

But how could indulgences "produce" money, to use Ranke's term?

The great Church of St. Peter was now under way; Julius had thrown himself into the project with characteristic enthusiasm, in Rome the dreams of Bramante and Michelangelo were being crystallized. The whole church was to participate in the creation of this magnificent pile. Those who had means were to contribute money, those who had none were to pray for the success of the enterprise. As the monks had in past generations gone through Europe preaching the crusades, so now they went among the people preaching the construction of Christendom's mighty altar. Whoever in any way contributed to so desirable an object did a good deed, and as a reward for that deed received an indulgence. The instructions of the popes were clear enough: the indulgence was to be granted to him who, having made a good confession and received absolution, should give to the fund for St. Peter's; or, if he had no means, should pray for the fortunate progress of the enterprise.

If, then, the greedy civil authorities were "appropriating" two-thirds of the contributions made for holy purposes, it may be conjectured that corruption would enter into the system. That it did so is quite evident from a study of Catholic authorities. The Jesuit writer whom I have quoted already says:

"Did any great abuse occur in connection with the indulgence preached by Tetzel and his companions? Yes. What we now call 'graft' was a pretty common abuse in Luther's time. It was perhaps almost as bad then as it is to-day. But it was a much greater scandal then than it is now, because many persons guilty of it were churchmen, and not merely city or state officials. The crime of simony—that is, selling sacred things for money or its equivalent—has often been a plague of the church. It has done a great amount of harm by getting unworthy men into sacred offices.

Then these unworthy bishops or cardinals disgraced their holy religion and caused those very scandals which Luther gave as a pretext for his reform. For instance, Albert, the archbishop of Mayence at the time we speak of, had become archbishop by simony; and when the indulgence of St. Peter's Church was preached, he strove to have one-third of the money collected in his province turned into his own pocket to reimburse him for the sum he had spent to get his office."

It was in 1500 that Germany took two-thirds of the funds raised for the erection of St. Peter's Church. Only seventeen years, and Luther will be preaching those tremendous Lenten sermons in Wittenberg. Three years, and Julius II will be pope. Maximilian I is emperor of Germany, Louis XII king of France, and the great Ferdinand has just driven the Moors out of Spain and reigns on the Iberian peninsula. In England Henry VII is on the throne; John II rules Denmark and Sweden. It was a period of strange psychological uneasiness; mighty impulses were stirring everywhere. The adventurous mind of Europe was reaching out over the world. Columbus had discovered the western continent beyond the Atlantic; soldiers and missionaries were already at work in the new lands, the former searching for treasure and the latter for souls.

In Rome St. Peter's was rising like the body of the Renaissance. What was the Rome of the time? Ranke says of it that it was a splendid city, indeed. "Here," he says, "the mechanic found employment, the artist honor, and safety was assured to all."

Julius II effected many changes: it was a different
community from that in which Cæsar Borgia had
swaggered with his tiger strength and tiger spirit, his
sword and dagger and poison, so short a time before.
A wise and just government, a market for the wares
and a field for the talent of every man, security for his
person and property and encouragement for his ge-
nius—such a city Pope Leo X received from the hands
of his warlike predecessor.

John de' Medici, son of Lorenzo the Magnificent,
boyhood friend of Ariosto, a brave soldier under
Julius before he was ordained a priest, a courtly,
learned, gracious man—such was the new pope.
Ranke says he was full of kindness and ready sym-
pathies. One ambassador writes home to his sovereign
that Leo is "a good man, avoiding disorders"; another
says in his despatches, "He is a scholar and a lover of
learning; a good priest, if he enjoys life." His election could not but increase the prestige of the Holy
City. Men of science and artists flocked there, sure
of the patronage of this enlightened pope. He was
passionately fond of music, and the poets and com-
posers of the day found no prince as generous as the
head of the church.

Meanwhile, as even monarchs must die, there are
new names in the royal directory of Europe. Henry
VIII has ascended the English throne. Maximilian
still rules the German empire, but in a short year he is
to give place to the great emperor Charles V of the
house of Austria, whose sceptre is to be supreme in
Austria, Germany, Spain, the Netherlands, and
Naples, conquest and fortunate marriages having

brought all these crowns to one head. The chivalrous Francis I is on the throne of France, in Denmark and Sweden there rules a butcher and tyrant, Christian II, who rids himself of his Swedish enemies by having them slain at a banquet, an incident execrated in Swedish history under the title of "The Bloody Bath." Gustavus Vasa is preparing to free Sweden from his thrall. One of the great lords of the German Empire is the elector Frederick of Saxony, the patron and friend of a daring and eloquent Augustinian monk, Martin Luther.

Enterprising gentlemen are these princes, all of them. Not a single royal breast in Europe but holds a boundless ambition. Not a single monarch of the lot who is not proud, imperious, impatient of check. Among them a Julius II might hold his own politically, but not a Leo X.

In spite of his birth and training, I doubt if Leo understood the political spirit of his age. The learning and the art, what illuminated the mind and stirred the love of beauty—these he knew well; but the coarser emotions and impulses that moved the powers remote from Rome were not within the circumference of his knowledge. He was learned in the direction of his tastes, and his tastes were not for practical politics. Even to the day of his death he was blind to the significance of the Lutheran movement—he thought it but a mere monkish quarrel in Germany between the Augustinian and the Dominican orders.

But what Leo failed to see the ambitious princes did not fail to see. "Throughout the whole period of time that we are contemplating," Ranke declares, "there was no assistance so much desired by the temporal sovereigns in their disputes with the popes as that of a spiritual opposition to their decrees. . . . The mere fact that so fearless a foe to the popedom had made his appearance, the very existence of such a phenomenon, was highly significant, and imparted to the person of the reformer *a decided political importance.* It was thus that Maximilian, the German emperor, considered it; nor would he permit injury of any kind to be offered to this monk; he caused him to be specially recommended to the Elector of Saxony— 'there might come a time when he would be needed' —and from that moment the influence of Luther increased day by day."

"The time when he would be needed" came, indeed; but Maximilian was dead: it was his successor Charles V who was to turn to political account the great reformer, although many a prince outside Germany and in Germany employed for his own purposes then and afterward the movement the doctor of Wittenberg shaped and launched. Leo devoted his life mainly to the encouragement of art and letters and the construction of St. Peter's. Political matters seem to have been a bother of which he rid himself with as little trouble as possible. He did drive the French out of Italy when his Swiss defeated the forces of Louis XII at Novara, but when the high-spirited Francis I swept back across the Alps and worsted the Swiss on the field of Marignano in 1515, the pope hastened to meet him at Bologna and to make that peace which gave to the French monarch the duchies of Parma and Placentia, and, what was more important, renewed the right of the nomination of French bishops. Toward the close of his pontificate Leo again took measures against the French, and it was in the midst of the celebration of the victory of the papal forces that a mortal sickness struck him down.

Meanwhile Luther's fierce protest against glaring abuses was rousing the German states. While the humanists hailed him gladly as a champion of intellectual freedom, and the churches in which he preached were crowded with the common people, who were thrilled by the thunderous eloquence which was in so great a degree his gift, the princes and nobles were taking advantage of the public opinion he created to divert to their own coffers the funds that had formerly gone to the church, and to add to their own domains the broad acres it had acquired. The nobility, and many priests and bishops, tasted absolute freedom and found it sweet: numbers of the Teutonic Knights followed the advice Luther gave them in his letter to the grand master of their monastic order, and took wives and church property at the same time. Where Luther's personal influence was felt, where that attribute which the phraseology of our day calls personal magnetism could exert its indefinable but mighty influence, there can be no doubt that the peasantry were also affected; but it is very doubtful if the Reformation made much progress at this time except among the princes, nobles, and schoolmen.

Macaulay says that its fiftieth year saw Protestantism at high tide, but it is plain that he was considering only its political extension, the area covered by those states in which it controlled the ruling powers. My own opinion is that its actual numerical strength among the common people was greater at a later period. Much has been said of the influence of the printing-press in stimulating the revolt, of the influence of that hurricane of pamphlets which the reformers let loose upon Europe; but it must be remembered that the illiterate were then the great majority, upon whom the printing-press could not have much influence. It was example and coercion that did the work in the lower ranks, the example of pastors to whom the people were accustomed to look for spiritual guidance, and the pressure of the secular powers whom they were accustomed to see enforcing the observance of religion.

Macaulay is right, however, with regard to the political power of the Protestant movement. The spoil of the church had created a new interest, and that interest was in the ruling class. It was that influence that now gave to Protestantism a very considerable political power. Charles V, although he never professed other than the Catholic faith, did not hesitate to use the conditions created by the Reformation as a club in his political complications with the Roman State. After the death of Leo, the cardinals elected as pope a bishop of the Netherlands who was famed all over Christendom for his intense piety and personal purity of life. His brief pontificate was saddened by the political difficulties of the Roman State and the successes of the Turkish arms. In France, Francis I was preparing to descend again upon Italy, and the Crescent achieved bloody triumphs at Belgrade and Rhodes. In the shadow of the coming storm he ended his days.

Giulio de' Medici, a nephew of Leo X, succeeded Adrian as pope. He assumed the name of Clement VII, and it was about his mitred head that the storm broke in all its fury. Although he had been a warm friend of Charles V, the plans of the latter with regard to the extension of the imperial power over Italy soon grieved the heart of the pontiff. Italy was filled with the Spanish forces of the emperor, and the Spanish pride was then at its height: they were arrogant warriors, indeed, who represented the imperial power to the exasperated Italians. Venice was becoming alarmed at the proximity of a too powerful and enterprising neighbor; everywhere the Italian princes were resentful of the oppression under which they lay. With the murmuring princes Clement entered into an understanding; the dream of a free Italy took possession of the Italian mind. General Pescara, the Italian-born Spaniard who commanded the forces of Charles, was approached, but he scornfully rejected the Italian advances and informed the emperor of the plans being matured. The revolt of Milan gave confirmation to his tidings, the imperial troops were driven back, Venice and Rome announced their combination, and from foreign states jealous of the power of Charles came promises of assistance. England, Switzerland, and France were to send their soldiers to the succor of Italy. Italian hope grew high and bright; it was believed that even without the aid of the friendly powers the object of the movement would be achieved; the reign of a second Julius was everywhere expected. Giberto expresses the feeling in Rome. "This war," he says, "is to decide whether Italy shall be free."

Meanwhile the princes of Germany are meeting at Spires. Ferdinand, duke of Austria, presides in the emperor's stead. Feeling against the pope runs high, the princes take advantage of it to bring forward the religious issue. Saxony, Hesse, and other principalities declare for Protestantism. In behalf of the emperor, Ferdinand signs a resolution decreeing that each prince shall decide for himself what the faith of his subjects shall be. Joyfully now the princes repay the imperial power; they give to Charles the troops and supplies he needs. Alva was afterward to let his Catholicity temper the rigor of warfare against a pope, but it was no such leader that Charles V sent forth against Clement VII. In November, 1526, George Frundberg crossed the Alps with a host of Lutheran *lanzknechts* who were to take their pay where they might find it, and the threat on Frundberg's lips was that when he got to Rome he would hang the pope.

The Italian resistance was but a mist the fiery hurricane blew away. Frundberg's progress through Italy was a series of easy successes. The promised aid from foreign sources was withheld, and only five hundred armed men awaited the charge of the fierce invaders outside the gates of the Holy City. Frundberg was stricken and helpless—a furious rage at some of his mutinous subordinates had burst a blood-vessel in his brain—and Bourbon led the Germans. The little band of defenders was overwhelmed in the first rushing charge of the Lutheran squadrons, who now pressed on to assail the poorly manned walls. With his foot on a scaling-ladder, Bourbon received his death-wound, and the leaderless horde, whose pay was to be the spoil of the richest city in the world, swept on to unchecked pillage in the great depository of all that was most splendid in art and most valuable in gold and gems. Treasure of incalculable worth fell into the hands of those rude invaders: the splendor of the Eternal City was submerged that day in an inundation from whose effects it took centuries to emerge. Thus died Pope Clement's dream of a free Italy bulwarking an unhampered church; thus did a German emperor use for his own purposes the physical force of the Reformation.

The physical church lay now in the mailed hand of a secular prince. Clement had stood siege in his castle awhile, but at last had surrendered to the emperor; and Charles rejoiced, as Philip the Fair of France had once rejoiced, in the prospect of shaping ecclesiastical policy to his personal ends. Clement was under no illusions, he felt the power and divined the purpose, and he resisted with all his strength the pressure Charles brought to bear on him to call a general council which under the circumstances must be wholly at the mercy of the victorious prince. Charles, on his side, was willing to make some concessions, particularly as they harmonized with his worldly policy. The Reformation had been used, but now the church was to be used; and if it was to be the instrument of imperial power—why, the stronger its influence the more effective an instrument would it make. Simultaneously, the peace with the pope was proclaimed and the outlawry of Luther decreed. Many thoughtful historians doubt the sincerity of Charles with regard to this last decree of the Diet of Worms. It is true that no effort was made by the imperial government to seek out Luther while the latter was concealed by powerful political friends whose understanding with Charles was excellent. The pope was informed that Luther was dead, and the report, gaining general circulation, reached the Germans in the form of an accusation of assassination against the agents of Rome.

Meanwhile the perplexities of Clement were driving him into an alliance with Francis, the old enemy of his house. The French king, while adhering to the old religion, was deep in combinations with the political powers of the new. He hoped to make them his instruments in holding the house of Austria in check, and with his concurrence the formidable Protestant leader, the landgrave Philip of Hesse, restored his duchy to the Duke of Wittenberg, whom Ferdinand of Austria had dispossessed. The duke promptly made Wittenberg Protestant, and Ferdinand as promptly surrendered his claim to it and made an alliance with the landgrave, much to the chagrin of the French monarch.

The powers of the North, no less than those of the South, found the religious movement of value. Gustavus Vasa drove the tyrant Christian out of Sweden and used the royal power his successful rebellion gave him to seize the church lands and church treasures and introduce Lutheranism as the state religion, so that his possession thereof might be considered proper and legitimate. The bloody-minded Christian did no less: he laid his hand on ecclesiastical property and made the new religion the state religion of Denmark with the bayonets of foreign mercenaries. Henry VIII of England, refused a divorce by Pope Clement, decreed a separation of the English church from that of Rome and constituted an ecclesiastical tribunal which would legitimize his union with fair Anne Boleyn. The Palatinate followed the example of other German principalities and embraced the teachings of Luther.

Everywhere the change in creed was accompanied by the pillage of church properties. A new and easy road to wealth had been opened to an impoverished aristocracy, and they trod it joyfully.

If the common people thought the ruling class had any idea of the extension of the right of private judgment below the aristocratic order—and beyond doubt there were places where they did so believe—they were soon to suffer a bloody disillusionment. The resolution of the Diet of Spires permitted each *prince* to determine the religious complexion of his province: it was by no means intended that each peasant and burgher should think for himself. The political power of the day could endure neither authority above nor freedom below; for if the peasants could take from the nobles what the nobles took from the church, where would the profit be? Thomas Münzer, the Lutheran pastor of Zwickau, found that private judgment had its social limitations, indeed: Luther himself cried out for the extermination of the revolting serfs whom

Münzer led in that merciless struggle written red in history as the Peasants' War; and when the last stronghold of the rebels had been taken and John of Leyden, the strange king of that strange kingdom, was in the hands of the Protestant powers, John and his associates in that Protestant movement were "killed with hot pincers" with full Protestant approval. Nor was it alone their own German nobles who thus sternly repressed the right of private judgment when those not of their order sought to exercise it. Wherever they went, the Protestant secular power killed them with cruelty: Henry VIII in England burned at the stake ten of the unfortunate Anabaptists.

Princes were guided with regard to religion almost entirely by political considerations, and these often of the most personal and selfish nature. Philip II of Spain was an ardent Catholic monarch. Why? Hilaire Belloc points out that Spain was the only country of Europe where Protestantism was absolutely unknown, and he attributes this fact to the other fact that when the Reformation came Spain still had a throbbing memory of its tremendous struggle to expel the Moors. It could still feel the tingle of handgrips with the Mohammedan; the old war-cries, "Jesu!" and "Maria!" for Spain, and "Allah il Allah!" for the Moors, still echoed over fields of national glory. The conflict had blended Catholic enthusiasm with the national spirit of the people. What chance would a monarch of an Austrian house have had with a martial people whose religion was indistinguishable from their patriotism, had he set his face against that religion? Charles V knew well what he was doing when he sent the German troops to war against the pope and left his splendid Spanish soldiers unemployed in that great enterprise.

In every land politics made use of religion. Philip found it convenient in Spain to be a Catholic champion. In England Henry had seized the church machinery to make it serve his headlong passion, but the passion and the means whereby he gratified it combined to produce political consequences of the gravest importance. It was not without difficulty that he and the school of politicians whose fortunes were based upon the service of his pleasures overthrew the old form of worship: Hallam tells us that foreign soldiers had to be employed to force the Protestant faith on the people of England. It was upon the death of Henry, however, that the matter took on a more definite political form. He had left three children— the princess Mary, daughter of Catherine of Aragon; the princess Elizabeth, daughter of Anne Boleyn; and Prince Edward, the son of Jane Seymour. Two of these, Elizabeth and Edward, the Catholic subjects considered illegitimate. But the band of courtiers and politicians who had enriched themselves at the expense of the ancient church had the most pressing reasons for keeping Mary from the throne; their wealth and even their personal safety depended upon the Protestant succession. Gathering around Lord Somerset, the brother of Jane Seymour and the uncle of her son, they elevated Edward VI to the throne. Against them the Catholic faction united, their hopes centred upon the princess Mary. They were ready when the boy king died, and before Elizabeth could be proclaimed, Mary had unfurled her banner and, supported by the Catholic leaders and a popular army, had taken her crown. And now the Protestant faction, out of court favor, organized its forces and planned for the elevation of Elizabeth. Joyfully they hailed her accession, enthusiastically they prepared to avenge themselves on their political foes. There seemed at first some little difficulty with the queen herself: her hatred of married priests, and other predilections not in accord with the Protestant spirit, indicate that she was not at heart a very cordial lover of the new religion, and it is doubtful if she would have served the purpose of the Protestant faction could she have made peace with Rome on her own terms. She demanded of the pope an acknowledgment of her legitimacy. Her right to the crown depended on that, and, when it was refused to her, the political necessities of her case compelled her to accept the leadership of the Protestant party.

But now that party had become the national party. Elizabeth's illegitimacy presumed the succession to lie in Mary, queen of Scotland and allied by marriage and by blood to France. The national spirit had borne with some irritation the influence of the Spaniard Philip as the husband of the late queen Mary, and it was not inclined to have any but an English monarch. Thus came the patriotism of England to reinforce that faction whose interest lay in the Protestant succession.

And nothing was left undone to strengthen the combination; every effort was made to create a public abhorrence of Rome. The wildest calumnies were preached, the baldest forgeries perpetrated; sedulously did the politicians labor until there was created that spirit of hatred which could endure no beauty and no joy because these things were held to be Romish and therefore abhorrent. The Catholic politicians fought as bitterly to offset this agitation, but in vain; the circumstances of the time conspired to make their task impossible. Philip of Spain, who disliked the English as much as they disliked him, meditated the conquest of the insular kingdom. The people rallied to the support of the Protestant leaders, whose fortunes were now the fortunes of England. They were assured that the proposed invasion was due to the machinations of Rome. Now while it is true that the pope hailed with joy a project which would, if successful, restore England to the church, it is true also that Philip had personal and political motives which would have stirred him if there had been no religious consideration at all. No more haughty monarch wore a crown, and there had been insults while he was in England that left old scores to settle. Then there were Drake and those bold marauders who made piracy the calling of an English gentleman at the expense of Spanish commerce. How bitter must have been the irritation of a proud and mighty prince whose treasure-ships were plundered and sunk in the very seas that Spanish enterprise had opened to the navigators of the world! The tongue we speak has carried down to us an admiration for those bold toll-takers of the wave, but in Spain at that time they were regarded as plain thieves and murderers, and the insular kingdom that sent them forth as a nest of pirates no more respectable than the states of the Barbary coast. Europe shared the impression of them held by Spain; Ranke speaks of them as the "bold corsairs" who gathered in to defend their island home when the Armada threatened it.

But although the Protestant party had gained a great advantage, there was still a powerful Catholic party whose traditions and machinery were later to pass into the Jacobite party, as in this Republic the machinery and traditions of the old Whig party passed into the Republican party; and the bitterness of the political struggle between the two generated a bitter prejudice which has been bequeathed to our country and our generation. It was necessary for the dominant faction to keep the "raw head and bloody bones" ever before the eyes of the people in order to insure their devotion to the "Protestant succession." When America was settled the battle was still on. French and Spanish America and English and Dutch America still had to fight it out.

But long before the Revolution the fight had ended; only the prejudice remained. The devotion of Catholic Maryland to the patriot cause, and the help of Catholic France, mitigated but did not eradicate it. Succeeding events have "softened" it, but it still remains. Although the storms of four centuries ago destroyed and dispersed "the Invincible Armada" in distant seas, the dread of it and the hate of it control the school policy of America to-day. The political rancor of the fifteenth century has power still to compel a nation believing in God and democracy to turn its youth over to materialism and Socialism. Between us and our best interests as a state rises the ghost of a Spanish king who died in 1598, and we cannot see through it.

CHAPTER VIII

THE DAGGERS THAT WERE NOT BLESSED

MEYERBEER'S grand opera, "The Huguenots," has an intensely dramatic scene. It pictures the Cardinal of Lorraine blessing the French daggers that were to do the bloody work of St. Bartholomew's Day. That scene, one of the most impressive in the brilliant opera, has had much to do with the quite general Protestant belief that the Catholic Church instigated, and through its agents carried out, the slaughter of Protestants in France that was begun in Paris on August 24, 1572.

From what historical authority, from what in the form of record or tradition, did Scribe, who wrote the libretto of "The Huguenots," take the inspiration for this great stage picture? No historian of that time, Protestant or Catholic, made mention of any such occurrence. The written record is that at the time of the massacre, and for some time before and some time after, the Cardinal of Lorraine was far from France: he was in Rome attending a conclave of cardinals assembled for the election of a pope. Whence, then, did Scribe get the idea of this scene? From the literature of the theatre, from another stage production, the frankly admitted invention of the Revolutionary poet Chénier, came this terrific arraignment that has excited the honest horror of millions who believe it to be based upon the facts of history. The play was

"Charles IX," presented for the first time in Paris in 1798, at which time Chénier published a "Dedicatory Address to the French People," containing this explanation:

"At the time of the massacre the Cardinal of Lorraine *was in Rome.* I do not think it is right to change history; but I think it is allowable, in an historical tragedy, to invent certain incidents, provided the privilege be used with moderation."

But the explanation is not read now, and, except by students of history, has been little read at any time; while deep in the souls of men has been printed the picture of the Catholic cardinal blessing the blades for the day of blood, and in their ears have rung his words:

"A humble and docile son of the immortal church, and made a priest of the living God by her hands, I am able to interpret the divine decrees. If your souls are filled with a burning zeal to devote themselves to the interests of Heaven, if you bring to murder religious hearts, you will accomplish a tremendous task. Serve well the God of nations, all of whose blessings I now shower upon you! Know that in heaven God now breaks the chain of your iniquities: by the God who inspires me, I declare the forgiveness of whatever crimes you have ever committed. When the church impressed on my soul her ineffaceable mark, she forbade me to shed even the most guilty blood: but I shall follow in your path, and in the name of the avenging God I shall direct your blows. Warriors, whom divine Providence is about to lead; ministers of justice, chosen by his prudence; it is now time to accomplish the eternal decrees. Bathe yourselves holily in the blood of the wicked!"

These words were never uttered by the great prelate of the house of Guise; there was no blessing of the daggers. In France, as elsewhere, the so-called "wars of religion" were caused by politics—by the selfish and corrupt politics of kingcraft, that were the same essentially as the politics of the Tweed Ring in New York City, and of other corrupt political cabals in other cities only too familiar to modern American thought. More than once, in the article dealing with the Huguenots, is this expressly stated by the American Cyclopædia, published in 1869, and edited by George Ripley and Charles A. Dana.

"The Reformation, which was far from being entirely religious even in Germany," says this work, "was much more the result of secular and local causes in France." And again, "It was during the reign of Henry II that the Huguenots gathered such strength as to entertain hopes of becoming the dominant political party."

Indeed, the political powers of France were at that time more than half Protestant; the younger branch of the reigning house of Bourbon was wholly so. It was in the masses of the population that Catholicity kept a predominating strength; the same peasant sentiment that later was to bar the popular and victorious Henry of Navarre from the throne until he bowed the knee in the Catholic Church made it the part of political wisdom for Francis I to adhere to the old church, at war though he might be with the Papal States and allied, as he was, with the Protestant powers outside his own kingdom. In the day of Francis, no court in Europe was as gay as that of his sister, the famous Margaret of Navarre. Around her was a revelling, witty, and anything but devout society: her ladies blushed and giggled over those tales of light love in which the keen but unclean mind of Boccaccio delighted; and the butt of every ribald joke was the monk or the sacraments of the church. From the first the sympathy of the vivacious Margaret went out to the assailants of the church. Her court became their refuge. Farel, who did so much to establish the Genevan state on the basis of the new theology, was one of her favorites; to her fled John Calvin when Cop's preaching in the Sorbonne of the sermon he wrote made flight from Paris the part of prudence for preacher and author. Here were brought up Jeanne d'Albret, the mother of Henry IV, and the Bourbons of the younger branch—Antoine, afterward a Navarrese king, and Louis, the Prince of Condé, soon to be the gallant military chieftain of the Protestant faction. These younger Bourbons could not but despise the physically and mentally weak children of Catherine de' Medici, who stood between them and the throne of France; they ever entertained the hope of gaining that mighty sceptre, and they bore a deadly hatred toward the Guises, whose matrimonial alliance with the older branch was productive of an influence in the government of the realm of which those bold and enterprising politicians took full measure of advantage.

In the reign of Henry II, the husband of Catherine de' Medici, this political force was gathering head. It found a ready ally in the queen, who was thoroughly in sympathy with the Rabelaisian humor of the court, in so far as it turned the church to ridicule, and was eager to get the Guises out of the way in order that she might sway, through the weakness of her son Francis, the government of France. For this beautiful and remarkable Florentine had but one passion, and that was for power. A fastidiousness or a political prudence kept her personally chaste, but she was quite willing to turn the moral lapses even of husband and son to the service of her cold policy; she shrank from no bloodshed if she conceived it to be in line with her purpose. She probably held all religion in contempt; it was more the novelty of the Lutheran creed than any feeling of sympathy with it, I think, that caused her to enliven her meals with Protestant sermons, as Santa Croce, the papal nuncio, complained in his reports.

Nor is it reasonable to think that this woman had any friendship for the younger branch of her husband's family, or any intention of allowing that branch to gain a decided ascendancy. The common sentiment that brought them together was their contempt for Catherine's sons, and their fear and hatred of the house of Guise. François, the head of that ducal family, was famous as a captain throughout Europe; to him and to his brother, the Cardinal of Lorraine, their niece Mary, wife of Francis II, turned for advice and protection. The young king's passion for the beautiful Stuart, who was later to reign so unhappily in Scotland and to lay her lovely head at the last on the block in England because of too plau-

sible a claim to the throne of that kingdom, maddened
Catherine, who found her influence nullified by that of
the valiant François. Of that politician she determined to rid herself by a bold stroke, for which the
strength and inclination of the younger Bourbons
promised to furnish the means. It was planned by
Catherine, by the King of Navarre, the Prince de
Condé, and the great Protestant lord Coligny, to cap-
ture and imprison the young king, slay the Duke of
Guise, and establish for the government of France a
regency council of Huguenot powers under the leadership of the queen mother.

This was the conspiracy of Amboise. Its exposure
put all the cards in the hands of the Guises—the
duke François and Lorraine were more than ever the
protectors and advisers of the monarch, and Catherine, without scruple, abandoned her Protestant allies
and professed a sudden and excessive detestation of
heretics and as sudden and remarkable a devotion to
the house of Guise. The duke did not press his advantage to the utmost; he was quite content that Francis
should know who the conspirators had been without
subjecting them to punishment. Condé he did humiliate by compelling him to look on without protest
while his own partisans were paying in blood the price
that Condé himself should have paid for that treason.

By this time the faith of the French Protestants
had been organized by Calvin, and already there was
bitterness between those who followed the French
doctor and those who accepted the Lutheran Confession of Augsburg. The princes of Navarre were the
political heads of the Calvinist movement, and the

Guises sought to weaken them by causing the toleration in France of Lutheran Protestantism. Bloody commotions in the Protestant ranks followed, and these disturbances of the peace of the kingdom did not increase the reputation of the Huguenots among the masses of Frenchmen. Condé was at the forefront of every armed uprising; he was arrested at Orléans, charged with high treason, and would undoubtedly have lost his head had it not been for the sudden death of Francis and the elevation to the throne of his brother, Charles IX.

For the moment Catherine's prospects brightened: no longer was Mary Stuart's white hand on the sceptre, no longer did her proud uncles exercise through her a dominating influence over the court. The first move of the new king was to pardon the foes of the house of Guise. Condé was no sooner free than he took the field at the head of his faction, and carried on open war until the Duke of Guise defeated him on the field of Drieux and took him prisoner.

Soon, however, was the great duke to pay the price of princely politics in those times. While he was conducting the siege of Orléans he was treacherously shot by a partisan of Admiral Coligny, and his family and the nation at large laid the blame of his assassination on the shoulders of the Protestant leader. His son, Henry of Lorraine, who was to take his place at the head of the house, saw him fall, and over his body swore an oath of vengeance against the admiral—an oath which he lost no opportunity of fulfilling.

The wavering policy of Charles, who swung like a pendulum back and forth, now inclining toward the

Guises and now toward the Huguenots, favored at this time the Protestant leaders. His edict of Amboise freed the imprisoned Condé, who took immediate advantage of his freedom to raise his banner once more and claim the throne. His mints printed coins bearing his effigy with the inscription, "Louis XIII, First Christian King of France." He very nearly succeeded in capturing the king and queen at Mieux, but the royal forces overcame him at St. Denis, and once more he was a prisoner. The peace of Longjumeau gave him his last opportunity to rebel; he fought with great bravery at Jarnac, and was shot by an officer of the Duke of Anjou.

Meanwhile the war went on and the Huguenots called to their aid German and English fellow-religionists, while the Guises began to receive support from Philip of Spain, who was hopeful of gaining France through their influence. Young Guise, who had received his baptism of fire in the war against the Turks in Hungary in his seventeenth year, pursued his vendetta relentlessly—at Jarnac and Moncontour his sword was reddened, and the great Coligny had to yield to his bitterest enemy at Poitiers. When Charles made the peace of St. Germain, Henry had to abandon public war for private vengeance, and the growing influence of the gallant Coligny with King Charles, the agreement that the two branches of the reigning house should be united by the marriage of Marguerite of Valois, sister of the king, to Henry of Navarre, the gallant son of Jeanne d'Albret, foreshadowed not only the ruin of the Guises but the relegation of the ambitious queen mother. Bitter, indeed, were the

hatreds that poisoned the atmosphere of the French
court in August of 1572, when a strange society assembled in Paris. Charles was for the time all for his
new friends; he called Coligny, whose grave courtesy
and noble bearing made a deep impression upon him,
his father. Henry of Guise beheld with hot anger in
his heart the elevation in esteem and influence of the
man he believed to be responsible for his father's assassination. Catherine, shoved to one side by the new
favorites, who hardly tried to dissemble their contempt for the king and their not unjustified suspicion
of those who surrounded him, took counsel with
Prince Henry, later to be the King of Poland and still
later Henry III of France, and between them was
hatched the plot for the killing of Coligny. It was
through young Guise they worked. Catherine's plan,
according to the conjectures of many historians, was
to have Guise commit the crime and then have him
beheaded for it; thus at one stroke ridding herself of
her two principal rivals. The conspiracy missed fire;
Guise's bravo wounded but did not kill Coligny, and
Charles IX was highly incensed at the attempt upon
the life of his new favorite. Catherine was now truly
alarmed; the Protestant nobles were in bitter and rebellious mood and kept their hands on their swords in
the royal halls, and Charles averted his face from her.
To save herself she and her allies forced themselves
into the presence of her son and alarmed him with the
charge of a Huguenot conspiracy aimed at his throne
and life. The bearing of the Huguenot leaders and
their record lent color to the tale, the unsteady mind
of the monarch was filled with terror, and he gave his

consent to what he called "the execution" of the leadders of the conspiracy. And young Guise was selected as the instrument of justice—Guise, whose heart was panting for Coligny's blood, whose future fortune depended on the suppression of the Huguenot power! He had made his preparations, he was ready. St. Bartholomew's Day blotched redly the history of France.

How many died? The estimates vary. De Thou says 30,000; La Popelinière, 20,000; Masson, 10,000; Lingard, 1,500. The author of the Huguenot martyrology gives an estimate of 30,000, but when he gives the figures by the cities and towns where outbreaks occurred they total 15,168, and when he attempts a roll of the martyrs of St. Bartholomew's Day, he brings forth the names of 768.

And now what part did the church play in all this? The story that flew through Protestant Europe was that the Catholic Church instigated it; that from Rome came the impulse; that the massacre was long in preparation, the marriage but a lure to gather together the heretics; that upon its consummation the pope ordered a *Te Deum* sung in celebration. But the record is all against this; there is the report of Salviati, the papal nuncio, written in cipher to the cardinal secretary of state, giving the details of Catherine's intrigue, and the request of the cardinal secretary for all the information that could be obtained. It is a plain story, such as any diplomatic agent might send to his distant government; there is nothing of jubilation in it, nothing to indicate that religion had the slightest part in it. There are the memoirs of Mar-

garet, Charles's sister, and the statement of the Duke
of Anjou, his brother, to his physician, all to the effect
that the plot was of sudden conception and due to the
growing ascendancy of Coligny and the fear entertained by Catherine and others of the consequences of
such an ascendancy. The *Te Deum* story has long
had its simple explanation. Rome was celebrating the
great victory of Lepanto over the Turks, and in the
midst of the celebration came the version of St. Bartholomew which Catherine's prudence invented; it
was merely that the king had escaped assassination at
the hands of heretics, and that Condé and Navarre
had abandoned the Protestant cause and accepted the
ancient church. For that was the *Te Deum* chanted
in Rome: the escape of a Catholic king and the accession of two powerful princes. Catherine's courier had
beaten the courier of Salviati in the race from Paris to
St. Peter's.

No sensible man need be informed of the danger of
letting loose a mob. The report that the rebel Huguenots had treacherously attacked the king went
through France, and those who are always willing to
profit by disorder joyfully took advantage of the opportunity. There is plenty of contemporary Protestant evidence to the effect that even Guise, when
Coligny and the leaders had fallen, rode through
Paris, checking the murderous spirit to which he himself had given rein; that everywhere respectable Catholics sheltered the hunted Protestants from the mob.
The Catholic bishop of Lisieux opened the cathedral
doors to the refugees, and throughout France monasteries and convents afforded them shelter. Twice

the Protestant forces had massacred the Catholics of Nîmes, but not a single Protestant was molested in that city. Catholic France, no less than Protestant Europe, was horrified at the effusion of blood: but Catholic France knew it was the result of a political intrigue; Protestant Europe charged it up to religious persecution. ·

And this is the final cipher despatch which Salviati, the nuncio, sent to Rome:

"Time will show whether there be any truth in all the other accounts which you may have read of the wounding and death of the admiral, that differ from what I wrote to you. The queen regent, having grown jealous of him, came to a resolution a few days before, and caused the arquebuse to be discharged at him without the knowledge of the king, but with the participation of the Duke of Anjou, of the Duchess of Nemours, and of her son, the Duke of Guise. Had he died immediately, no one else would have perished. But he did not die, and they began to expect some great evil; wherefore, closeting themselves in consultation with the king, they determined to throw shame aside, and to cause him [Coligny] to be assassinated with the others; a determination which was carried into execution that very night."

The house of Guise was again in the ascendant and it was to maintain this ascendancy for many a year of bloody strife in France. Henry, its head, now known as Le Balafré because of a scar that a wound had left upon his face, cemented its power by his military achievements and by the formation in 1576—four years after St. Bartholomew—of the Cath-

[164]

olic League.   Charles IX was dead—some say he died
of remorse, and some say he died of consumption—
and Henry III had come back from Poland to take the
crown of France.   The massacre of 1572, in which he
played a more effective part than did Charles, never
weighed uncomfortably upon his conscience after his
accession to the throne.   He resented the power of
Balafré and his house, and soon there was an open
rupture and France became the theatre of the so-
called "War of the Three Henrys."   There had grown
up at Guise's side his younger brother Mayenne, a
warrior of the same type, and, with the League devoted to them, these two brothers were more than a
match for Henry of France and Henry of Navarre.
Having defeated an army of Germans sent into
France to aid the enemies of the League, Guise entered Paris boldly and the whole population rose for
him on the "Day of the Barricades."   The king was
beleaguered in the Louvre; the city was in the
hands of his great vassal.   Guise's followers would
have proclaimed him king but he waved the crown
from him.

The States General were convoked, and at their
stormy sessions Balafré demanded the royal appointment as high constable and general of the kingdom.
It was quite evident that the Parliament was in his
favor, and the king resolved on the Machiavellian expedient.   Guise was treacherously slain by his order
in the council-room, and the same day the Cardinal of
Lorraine was murdered in prison.

But there was still a survivor of that lion brood:
Mayenne escaped the king's assassins, and Henry was

forced to seek safety in the camp of the King of Navarre. The Leaguers and the Huguenots again clashed with varying fortune, and at last the camp of the two kings was pitched outside the gates of Paris, which was held by the Duke of Mayenne. In the camp Henry acknowledged Navarre as his heir, but informed him that he would never occupy the throne until he became a Catholic. That this information was not despised by the Navarrese, when Henry III was assassinated and his right by birth to the crown unquestioned, is shown in his correspondence with the popes. In these negotiations also is the evidence of the political nature of these wars. The possibility of a reconciliation between Henry IV and the church enraged Philip II, and his agents at Rome and in France indulged in violent attacks on Pope Sixtus for entering into negotiations with Henry. Cardinal Cajetan, the Spaniard who was papal legate to the League, was so active in his opposition to the legiti-mate heir that the pope wrote to him, threatening him with severe penalties if he did not cease to act as the legate of Philip II and remember that it was the pope he represented in France. Mayenne, striving valiantly still against destiny, wrote to the pope, asking for men and arms, and begging him to support the League not only against Henry but against Philip, who was now no more desirous of a complete victory for the Leaguers than of a determinative triumph by Navarre. But France was weary of strife, and Henry's attachment to Protestantism was not strong. The king embraced the ancient faith, and France accepted the king; and the Huguenots thereupon ceased to be a considerable force in the political affairs of France.

Here again we find the political influences, the intrigues of princes, lighting the fires of bigotry to serve the purposes of politics. The politicians of a later day have other shibboleths, but similar methods. They generate hatred as the drivers of a locomotive generate steam; it is the force they need to accomplish their purpose. How long was the bitterness of the Civil War kept alive here, after the death of Lincoln, the forgiver, by cheap politicians who found profit to themselves in the waving of "the bloody shirt"? Have the demagogues of to-day forgotten the art—isn't the fomentation of class hatred the main occupation of more than half the ambitious and conscienceless self-glorifiers who so largely figure and loudly sound in the public life of our day? The form is changed, but not the substance. Ballots have to a large extent taken the place of blades, and an admixture of many creeds in the voting population has made the old shibboleths inconvenient for the vote-catchers; but they still generate hate, they still seek spoil through destruction. It is a very old business, this of making profit out of the public. It doesn't belong to the moderns of America alone; every land and every age has had it: it was in the Greek cities and in the Roman Republic, it was in the Italian life and the German life of the middle ages, it was in the Catholic League in France and the "Protestant Boys" of England.

Politics put its impress on the Reformation by the nationalization of the churches. Henry VIII defined the Church of England. The Lords of the Covenant

defined the Church of Scotland.   And these names did
not signify merely the location of the particular part
of a universal church, as did the terms "the Church of
Alexandria" and "the Church of Rome" among the
early Christians.   They meant churches with peculiarities of rite and dogma; the geographical limita-
tion of a divine revelation. Even among the Germanic
and Scandinavian states, where the acceptance of the
Lutheran form preserved a surface uniformity of
ritual and creed, there were national modifications inseparable from a complete ecclesiastical subserviency
to the national ruler.

It may be true that the right of private judgment
emerged from the Reformation, but it was a terrible
gauntlet it had to run before it emerged. Burned and
bloodied it was by Protestant no less than by Catholic
hands.   Draper quotes a Venetian envoy's report to
the effect that in the Netherlands and in Friesland
30,000 suffered death for Anabaptist opinions.   The
"Six Articles" of Henry VIII are still known in English history as "the Bloody Six," the name bestowed
upon them by the Tudor king's Catholic subjects; and
his daughter Mary is still remembered by the name
"Bloody Mary," which the Protestant subjects of her
time bestowed upon her. John Calvin could still bring
to the slow fire Michael Servetus, who preached a
Protestantism differing from his own only as his own
differed from that of Luther and Melanchthon.

And we have let politicians tell us these were the
fruits of religious controversy! We have accepted it
as true that they and many another bloody deed—that
all the persecution and all the cruelty—were caused

by religion. And it isn't true. Not a single instance
of so-called religious persecution that I have examined did not have a sufficient political reason.   There
was Catholic hatred in Ireland for the Protestants
because of the massacres by Elizabeth's Protestant
soldiery.   Spenser, the English poet,. who accompanied that soldiery, tells what was done: "In a short
space there was none almost [of the Catholics] left;
and a most populous and pleasant country was suddenly void of man and beast."   Was this wholesale
slaughter due to Elizabeth's zeal for the right of private interpretation?   Spenser answers our question;
he tells us he got, as his share, 3000 acres of the confiscated land of the slain Irish.   The Scottish lords
committed murder in the very presence of their Catholic queen.   Was it in protest against "the sale of indulgences"?

Henry VIII's "Six Articles"—what real care had
he for them? But he was a *king*, no subject might
gainsay *him;* it was for.lèse-majesté, for daring even
to disagree with what he did not himself believe but
said they must believe, that by the stake and the axe
they died by whom his religious decrees were called
"the Bloody Six."

And Mary was the very centre of a bitter political
battle—around her a band of politicians seeking vengeance for the wrongs of the previous reigns, at her
side a weathercock theologian, loyal to any faith that
might be the fashion. Against her were the politicians who had been turned out of power at her accession. Even then she checked the persecutors until
actual rebellions on the part of the Protestant faction

endangered her throne: not until Wyatt's abortive revolt were her partisans permitted to punish her political enemies.

The Servetus affair? Calvin was fighting the Libertines—the party which had that name in Germany and in Geneva—fighting them for political power with the aid of Frenchmen who flocked into Geneva, and his political enemies endeavored to make use of Servetus against him. It was for that Servetus died.

No matter how pure the spirit of any of the religious movements of those days, politics placed its cruel hand upon them, seized them, directed them to ends altogether irreligious. This is what a Protestant churchman thinks of it:

"Where Protestantism was an idea only, as in France or Italy," says Bishop Stubbs, "it was crushed out by the Inquisition; where, in conjunction with political power and sustained by ecclesiastical confiscation, it became a physical force, there it was lasting. It is not a pleasant view to take of the doctrinal change to see that where the movements toward it were pure and unworldly it failed; where it was seconded by territorial greed and political animosity it succeeded. . . . The instruments by which it was accomplished were despotic monarchs, unprincipled ministers, a rapacious aristocracy, and venal, slavish parliaments."

In closing this chapter, we may look back with some profit, I think, upon those which have preceded it, and give form to the conclusions they all justify. We have endeavored to deal with those incidents in the history of the Catholic Church which have been most productive of prejudice and which have revealed the interplay of internal and external influences—the relationships of church and state. Throughout all of them there is manifest a continuous conflict; on one side secular politics, on the other a religious aspiration for freedom of action. Sometimes on the part of the churchmen there are means employed which shock our sense of right; but always on the part of the opposing secular powers are such means employed. If we look back over the history of the church organization we see sometimes a misuse of power, sometimes a human ambition, sometimes shocking lapses from virtue on the part of high ecclesiastics. But if we look back over the history of secular politics, how utterly foul and cruel and murderous is the retrospect? What has secular politics to offer of good that was not impressed upon it by the church; what has the church to show of bad that was not due to the operations of secular politics? The tendency of the religious principle in the worst of times has been exalting and civilizing; the tendency of the other principle has been ever debasing and brutalizing. And to-day, when the politicians of the new school, when the special pleaders for an atheist school and an atheist age, turn to church history for illustrations of the injustice of the church and its evil effect upon social organization, they abstain from calling attention to the history of the thing they propose to substitute for religion in the life of men. They say that in past ages popes were bad, but dare they say that in the past ages worldly human government was not a thousand times more evil than the worst of the bad popes? Patrick Henry said the light of experience was the only lamp we had, but he meant the light of all experience, I think, not the light of a carefully selected part of experience.

The whole object of what I have written will be lost if this small work is considered as anything in the nature of Catholic apologetics. That church has her own apologists far more learned and far more eloquent. But that church has not a mere man of business apart from her own communion and therefore not predisposed in her favor, and it is the conclusion of such a man after a study of some historical events that I wish to set down here. It is quite possible to differ with the Catholic Church upon points of doctrine without accepting as true every fable that political animosity has invented to discredit it. We shall all be better Protestants, I think, for being fair. It is by no means necessary to my Methodism or another's Presbyterianism that we shall believe there was a Pope Joan, when there was not a Pope Joan; that we shall believe a religious spirit was responsible for St. Bartholomew's massacre when the real impelling force was secular and political. Nor need a man be now unduly excited over the right of Henry VIII to a divorce, or the question of Tudor or Stuart on the English throne, to be a devout and righteous member of the Church of England. Those old questions have hardened into history; they are no longer questions, they are facts. Mary Stuart and Elizabeth Tudor have gone to God, who has judged between them, doubtless; the Guises and the younger Bourbons—

and the older, too—have long since been laid in sepulchre; Philip II is of less real importance than little Johnnie Jones who is playing outside the window. Let them all go; we have problems enough of our own without clinging to those we can never solve because the Lord in his own way solved them long before we were born. Let us not forget the past, but let us look at the past as we look at the present: let us bury its prejudices with its dead; its political animosities with its politicians. The Church of God is made up of human beings; its inspiration and authority are divine. And humanity has been weak even in the Church of God, but immeasurably weaker outside it. That is the lesson of the history of the church and the states with which it has held a relationship.

Finally, is it reasonable to suppose that a church which has had experiences so unfortunate with state connections, should still desire them? In Italy there is still a desire for a restoration of the ancient political right of sovereignty; but the desire of Pius X is simply the desire of Zachary and his immediate successors in the days of Luitprand and Pepin, of Gregory in the days of the Germanic Empire, and Boniface in the days of Philip the Fair—a desire for a political shelter for a free church. The concordats, the concessions, the secular nomination for, or confirmation of, episcopal appointments: these are what "church and state" mean to the Catholic Church, and these things that church has hated historically and hates to-day. They are passing, and the church is glad. No more may a cardinal in conclave act as a vetoing agent of his political sovereign; the present pontiff has set his face and his word against the last faint shadow of secular interference. He has taken advantage of the public opinion of the twentieth century to reassert an ancient right fought for by his predecessors against oppressive external influences since that remote hour in which Constantine gave official recognition to the Christian church.

It has been charged against the Catholic Church that it shuts its eyes always to the changes in the world of men that come with the running generations, but this also is a misconception. No change has ever come over the world in all the long term of the pontifical succession which she has not adapted to her purpose. When they speak of an unchanging church it is of the doctrine they speak, of the deposit of truth which she boasts of carrying unchanged through all the vicissitudes of the troubled centuries. It is not the attitude of the church organization toward secular society. That attitude has ever been a changing one; it has conformed ever to the conditions of human life with which it had to deal; it fitted the catacombs, it fitted the court of the Cæsars, it fitted the Church State, it fitted the enlarged world that the enterprise of Columbus and Magellan and Da Gama gave to the activities of mankind; it fitted feudalism and monarchism and democracy each in its turn.

That is why Macaulay could write in 1840, long after the Reformation, but not so long after the French Revolution:

"The Papacy remains, not in decay, not a mere antique, but full of life and useful vigor. The Catholic Church is still sending forth to the farthest end of the world missionaries as zealous as those who landed in Kent with Augustine, and still confronting kings with the same spirit with which she confronted Attila. . . . Nor do we see any sign which indicates that the term of her long dominion is approaching. She saw the commencement of all the governments and of all the ecclesiastical establishments that now exist in the world; and we feel no assurance that she is not destined to see the end of them all. She was great and respected before the Saxon had set foot on Britain, before the Frank had passed the Rhine, when Grecian eloquence still flourished in Antioch, when idols were still worshiped in the temples of Mecca. And she may still exist in undiminished vigor when some traveller from New Zealand shall, in the midst of a vast solitude, take his stand on a broken arch of London Bridge to sketch the ruins of St. Paul's."

Three score and ten years of crowded human history, of most marvellous material achievement, of tremendous political vicissitude and immeasurable extensions of the field of knowledge in the realm of physical science; three score and ten such momentous years have contributed their amazing dynamics to the onward march of mankind, and is there yet any sign of diminishing power in this ancient church? Is she not fitting herself to the swiftly moving procession with all her ancient facility, and from each rapidly forming condition drawing an increase of power? Not that she veers with every shift of the breeze or bends her head to every ripple on the surface of the sea. Her pontiffs and priests have suffered in person, her ancient estates have been stripped from her—these have been incidents of her progress; but in the large view the church herself has prospered, has ever kept her course. And as Macaulay found her flourishing seventy years ago, despite conditions the world conceived to be adverse, so we find her to-day flourishing in the freedom of our American Republic and rejoicing greatly in the separation of church and state. Time and again, in his sermons to his own people and in his published works, Cardinal Gibbons has expressed the complete satisfaction of his church with the conditions which the wisdom of the fathers of the Republic provided for our American people. Listen to a prelate of the Catholic Church on this point! This is what Archbishop Blenk of New Orleans said in a sermon preached during the exercises in celebration of Cardinal Gibbons's golden jubilee and published in the New York *Sun* of October 11, 1911:

"Religion here is untrammelled, thanks to our separation of church and state; and whatever the future may bring, we would desire no change here in the relations of church and state. That is one lesson surely taught us by European history, and bitterly driven home by the events of our day. No meddling official has a veto power over our preaching. No bureaucrat, more or less hostile to religion, draws up the list of names from which our bishops are chosen. The Holy Father's counsel or legislative acts need no indorsement of potentates before they may cross our borders. Our pastors are supported by the love and generosity of believing congregations, and not by the stipends of a government. . . . Separation here is a real separation, not spoliation, not conspiracy to lessen the church's influence, nor restriction upon her liberty of action and liberty of teaching, nor tyrannical denial of the ministrations of religion to those who leave home to serve their country in army and navy. It means perfect freedom for church and state, each in its own sphere; but here, as there has been no divorce, there is no legacy of bitterness. On the friendliest of terms, neither has any desire for a closer union. The church here knows it can better do its work apart; it is freer and therefore more powerful, and, being unpaid by the state, and independent, it can uphold law and order without giving to any one an excuse to suspect its motives."

If in the brief and incomplete study of the past that has occupied these chapters, I have shown that what we have regarded here as religious prejudice is based very largely upon falsehood, and is the daughter less of doctrinal disagreement than of the corrupt politics of long ago; that the Catholic Church less than any other church, perhaps, desires a union of church and state; that, in any event, under modern conditions such a union is utterly impossible—if I have shown these things, then I may close this branch of my work and proceed to the consideration of the problem with which it is most concerned.

CHAPTER IX

THE PURPOSE OF THE SCHOOL

WHAT is Education? What is its purpose? Why are there so many school-houses, so many teachers, why so vast an expenditure in money, so extensive and complicate an organization, devoted to teaching the child? There never was an age that did not know education; never a tribe, savage or civilized, a part of whose social life did not consist of the systematic training of the young.

I have just read a book by Paul Monroe, Ph.D., who was professor of the History of Education at Columbia. It is entitled *A Brief Course in the History of Education.* In this book Professor Monroe traces the story of educational effort from primitive times to the present day, through all its varying fashions. He records the different theories men have held with regard to it, the mutations of form and content, the peculiarities of the succeeding schools. He elucidates the views of the authorities on the subject whose views are of record. They are varied enough. They were pagans, Christians, Catholics, Protestants, atheists; they were nominalists and realists, sense-realists and naturalists, formalists, humanists, and social-realists; Aristotelians, Schoolmen, Ciceronians; they were conservatives and radicals, Lutherans and Jesuits, ecclesiastics and Encyclopedists. In everything but one have they differed. There is one point upon which they all centred. From the early Hebrews and Greeks to the recognized modern authorities, there is a thread of agreement that holds a true course. There is one straight-edge that can be laid down upon the history of education from the beginning to now, and it will touch every great teacher from Plato to Pestalozzi, from Moses to Dr. Eliot. Differ as they may and do as to method, they all hold that the purpose of education is to make a good man. By whatever path, Virtue is the goal. By whatever method, the end is Righteousness. In all the long record there is no note of dissent upon this; in every system advanced everything else is secondary to the development of the moral character.

Before going back to the ancient thought on this subject it may be well to consider such primitive customs as savage life still extant, or but recently extinct, can exemplify. They give us some light; they show the same underlying purpose, the same all-pervasive principle. Fundamentally their conception of education is what ours is: it has its utilitarian side and its moral complement. The savage tribes teach their boys to hunt and fish, to fashion implements of war and chase, to build shelters and make clothing, just as we teach ours to read and write and figure, and in some cases to use their hands and brains in mechanical work. The savage lad is taught to take a living from his environment; the child of civilization, to earn a living in his. But this is not all: even among the savage tribes is the dim perception of a further need. The soul has its necessities; a man must be something more than strong and skilful in war and chase in order to be a useful member of the tribe. Human nature is nowhere without some moral idea, and the savage instinctively feels the need of inspiration: he must learn to endure without flinching, to fight without fearing, to reverence the old, to worship the spirits his fathers worshiped. Therefore the schooling of the youth, the exercises attendant upon his initiation into the adult tribal society, are conducted by the priesthood around the totem-pole. The groping of the unenlightened mind toward the truth; the natural phenomena personified in sun-gods and air-gods and wood-gods and river-gods, which are the symbols through which the dark, uncultured soul strives to express its vague but ever-present conception of a Creative Controlling Power—these are the things that affect his education. Far from civilization, where the intellect hardly throbs, where there has been no revelation and is no light, some mysterious power weds these two things— the secular education and the religious aspiration. The affinitive quality asserts itself with the force of a natural law. This education, Mr. Monroe says, has a moral value. It is not enough that the lad shall be a useful member of his tribe: he is "taught to be a *good* member of the tribe."

We shall pass over the educational system of the ancient Hebrews, whose public schools—of which they had many before the time of Christ—were informed, as was all their social life, by the spirit of their revealed religion, and see what the historian finds among the ancient Greeks. Here there was no revealed religion, no authoritative moral code. They had had to form their own religion, as did the savage tribes; but their keen minds had approximated the truth, their greater thinkers had reasoned a God from the natural evidences of His Being. Unaided, their logic had postulated a Supreme Intelligence morally perfect. But that was their logic at its best. The Greek mind of a lower order might in the vague Zeus mistily perceive the outlines of God, but it naturally thought of supernatural power in terms of its highly developed æsthetic sense: its familiar deities were the personifications of Power and Speed and Beauty— with these it peopled its heaven. Consequently there was an indistinct and indirect moral impulse, which did indeed predominate as an educational motive, but which lacked the compelling force of an authoritative moral commandment. It is for this reason that Mr. Monroe regards the Greek educational period as of great interest to modern American students. These are the words in which he points out the resemblance of educational conditions here and now to educational conditions there and then:

"Since the aim of education, as *limited* in the work of the American schools of to-day, must eliminate the religious element, it can find no *higher* purpose than that of determining for each individual the things in this life that are best worth living for."

In passing may I call attention to the two words I have italicized and their connotation that our education is a limited and an inferior education? They are valuable as an unconscious expression of the thought of an expert.

A limited and an inferior educational system the ancient Greeks had then, although they recognized

the need of something better and were seeking for it
ever. Aristotle declared the aim of education to be
goodness. There were two kinds of goodness, he
thought, goodness of intellect and goodness of character, and with regard to the latter he said: "Virtue
does not consist in the mere knowledge of the good,
but in the functioning of this knowledge." Socrates
and Plato held the same thought with regard to the
purpose of education: it must always be moral. And
the Greeks, reaching out for some moral staff on
which to lean, adopted various expedients: they
taught youths to emulate the virtues of their elders,
of the great men of the state; they provided the student with an "inspirer" whose name suggests his
office. But, lacking the authoritative moral code,
what was the result? How did their system, in which
Mr. Monroe sees so great a resemblance to our own,
work? This is his conclusion: "The ethical motive
among the masses of the people was not sufficiently
developed to prevent the toleration of many customs
abhorrent to modern times." He tells us what these
customs were—the debasement of women, the exposure of undesirable children so that they might
perish, the enslavement of nine-tenths of the population—these were some; and one is startled when he
thinks of what we have already upon us in the wave
of women politicians, professors of eugenics and promoters of Socialism—startled at the evidence of similar causes and similar effects. But it stops not there,
it goes further, and again we find modern developments keeping step with the ancient developments:
"Moreover, the Greek versatility bordered on the in-

sincere, even the dishonest, while their light-heartedness often became frivolity and licentiousness."

Possibly when Professor Monroe wrote his book the influence behind the secularization which he notes was not as clearly defined as it has since become, for he does not seem to consider that the pure socialism of the Spartan system had that particular interest for American educators which he found in the uninspired ethics of Grecian education elsewhere. Let me here remark, in order that the argumentative thread of this chapter shall remain unbroken, that even in Lacedæmon the purpose of education was moral. It was even more disciplinary in its motive and its operation than the monastic schools of the dark ages, there was a compelling force of the most direct and intimate nature behind its every precept. From the day the Spartan was born until the day he died, external influences channelled his life, his path was sharply defined.

"This resulted," Monroe says, "in the most perfect example of a socialistic state, and the most extreme case of government control of education, with emphasis upon the educational functions of various social institutions. In fact, society itself became a school in which every adult member was expected to participate, as an important duty of citizenship, in the education of the young Spartan."

It may be pointed out, however, that the socialistic system of the Spartans was something that was forced on them; that it was considered as a means of defense against hostile tribes by whom the state was surrounded; that its motive was military and its discipline therefore strict. The idea of the Spartan statesman was not to make happier the lot of the individual, to increase his material wealth and minister to his material comfort, but to make him a good soldier; and therefore a moral code, a strict, abstemious, laborious life, was necessary to the very purpose of the institution. This consideration has a bearing of the utmost weight upon the question Mr. Monroe asks and answers. He says their experience furnishes an affirmative answer to the question, Can morals be taught? Does it? The question is very interesting; it has been raised by the teachers of the ethical culture school; it is the principle of Dr. Eliot's theories with regard to education. Let us see, then, what it all amounted to ultimately. It cannot be denied that it kept the Lacedæmonians physically strong and nationally powerful for many years, but does it follow that it would do the same to-day for Americans? Would it have stood up in Sparta for any time at all had not hostile spears glistened on every frontier so that relaxation would have meant destruction to the state? Even then, would it have held together, had it not been for the fact that there was no private life, that every man lived day and night in the public view and according to a schedule prescribed by a strict and ever vigilant government? The Spartan might sin but he could not sin in secret, nor could he sin against the code established without the certainty of swift and severe punishment. But even with all this, what was the fruit of the tree, what was the effect of their system upon the moral character of this strange people?

"It must be admitted, however," Monroe says, "that while the Spartans' moral training conserved certain elemental virtues, its effects morally as well as physically had a certain hardening, even brutalizing, tendency."

So that is what it all ends in. That is the best ancient history can do in the way of an affirmative answer to the question, Can morals be taught?

The Roman people, the most wonderful of all the ancients, did not deviate from the line of moral purpose in their educational work. Sober, strong, practical people, less acute mentally but of a nobler order morally than the Greeks whose civilization they borrowed, they taught sobriety and reverence to their young; they held two sublime conceptions—justice and duty. In them more than in any other of the unenlightened peoples who flourished before the dawn of Christianity, a natural morality was developed. They were very practical men, their morality was for every-day use, they endeavored to make justice and duty less abstractions than rules of living. They were utilitarians, but utilitarians of the highest order, and they had developed a natural code of moral laws which received supernatural authority when Christianity came to make light what had been dark in the ways of men.

There will hardly be any question as to the purpose of the Christian schools. The fathers of the church might differ as to whether the learning of the pagan world was conducive to a virtuous character, but that a virtuous character was the end of all educational effort was never doubted. It was not questioned by

the scholastics, who endeavored to bring back some
of the ancient culture, by the humanists, by the students of the dawn years of the second millennium, in
whose hearts throbbed the first faint pulses of the
Renaissance.

Education took on a new form and color, but the
old motive persisted. The new intellectual period had
begun with the Holy Roman Empire. Charlemagne
was the first of the great Western patrons of learning;
his founder of schools, Alcuin, was an abbot of the
Christian church. St. Boniface, who founded schools
throughout Gaul and Germany, was another high ec-
clesiastic. For centuries yet the only teachers were to
be priests; but even when the lay schools began to be
more numerous, there was no departure from the old
basic idea, the precepts of religion were still the chief
part of the curriculum. Vittorio da Feltra, who established his famous school at Mantua in the closing
years of the fourteenth century, is called the first of
the modern schoolmasters. He declared that in his
system, "above all, moral and Christian influences
were strongly emphasized." Nor did the intellectual
ferment of the Reformation make any change in this
central idea. The humanists had never entertained
the suggestion that there could be other than a moral
purpose in education. Erasmus, the greatest of them,
held that "the moral purpose in education should ever
be emphasized, and a study of religious literature and
religious services should be a part of all training."
Nor were the Protestant leaders of different thought.
Imagine the amazement with which Luther would
have listened to a suggestion that religion be divorced

from education; think of Melanchthon, or Calvin, dreaming of such a possibility as a godless school!

John Milton the Puritan, the great poet, prescribes, among the subjects of study, "moral training, history, theology, church history." Comenius declared, "The ultimate end of man is beyond this life. . . . This life is but the preparation for eternity."

John Locke, the philosopher, adds this to the chorus: " 'Tis Virtue then, direct Virtue, which is the hard and valuable part to be aimed at in education, and not a forward pertness and any little arts of shifting."

And so the centuries roll on, and they have only one voice on this matter. The Encyclopedists take possession of the fashionable thought of France, and Rousseau writes his great work on education—*Émile*. "Now," says he, "his education is to be strictly moral and religious." This is the Rousseau who wrote *The Social Contract*, who even more than Voltaire "made the Revolution" in the thought of Napoleon and others. From Rousseau the thread leads to Pestalozzi, who brings us to modern thought and modern method. "In Europe," deplores Pestalozzi, "the culture of the people has become vain babbling, as fatal to faith as to true knowledge; an instruction of mere words which contain a little dreaming and show, which cannot give us the calm wisdom of faith and love, but on the contrary leads us to unbelief and superstition. . . ." Herbart says, "The one and whole work of education may be summed up in the concept—morality." And Froebel speaks to us next; in his *Education of Man* he says, "All things have come from the Divine Unit, from God, and have their origin in the Divine Unity alone." And this is Huxley's description of an educated man: " . . . The servant of a tender conscience who has learned to love all beauty in nature or art, to hate all vileness, and to respect others as himself." Less clear in expression, but of the same thought, is Professor James when he says education is "the organization of acquired habits of action such as will fit the individual to his physical and social environment"; and Professor Horne says, "Education is the superior adjustment of a physically and mentally developed conscious human being to his intellectual, emotional, and volitional environment." This last is merely the slang of the specialist for what an old Irishwoman better expressed when she said, "I'm sending Mickey to school to make a good man of him."

I might go on quoting indefinitely, but it is needless. Even the Nationalists, the Socialists, the Ferrerists, I take it, believe that the main and important purpose of schooling is to develop the moral character. The experience of humanity from the earliest times has taught but one lesson on this point: the moral results are the touchstone of the system—if a school does not make its pupils better men, then it is a failure. Leaving out of the question altogether the religious conception of man's creation and destiny, looking to human experience only, we find that the moral life is the only social safeguard; a prosperous and happy immoral people is inconceivable. States have stood up against external hostile influences, have persisted through material poverty, have survived even ignorance, but their morality has always been the very fibre of them, its decadence is always the forerunner of political disaster.

It is worth while noting the effect of the moral objective in education upon its utilitarian efficacy. And when we meet this question we uncover one of the paradoxes of human experience. Wherever the moral purpose of education is emphasized, the utilitarian purpose is well served; wherever the utilitarian purpose is emphasized neither is well served. Not to teach mathematics, but to teach morality, is the best way to make mathematicians. That is the way it has worked out. Take the monastic schools of the "dark ages." First let us make plain what we mean by the "dark ages." The name has been applied, strangely enough, to that period in history when there began to be a diffusion of light. The Greek civilization was luminous, it is true, but the light shone like a single star in a black sky. The diameter of civilization was short, indeed. The circle of light comprehended but a few square miles of the earth's surface lying around the eastern end of the Mediterranean Sea. Beyond that small circumference were vast black wildernesses. Toward the Orient was the faint afterglow of prehistoric civilizations. Africa lay to the south, in a night that has persisted unto this generation. America was in the deepest shadow, relieved only by a glimmer, perhaps, where the Aztecs, or the Toltecs, or the sun-worshiping Incas were lighting their feeble intellectual lamps. In Europe, save for that patch on the Mediterranean shore, the sons of Japhet walked in gloom. Nor was the Greek civilization of any depth. When it was purely Greek and at its brightest, it was but a surface glow. One-tenth of the Greeks were enlightened and free, nine-tenths of them the most abject and ignorant of slaves. The extension of that civilization to Rome deepened it slightly, but it became less brilliant as it was diffused over a larger area. To some extent the enterprise and valor of the Romans spread it north and west, but it gave only a faint radiance then—its pristine brilliancy was gone forever.

The illumination of the world was a task demanding a purer and a stronger light, and Christianity furnished the torch. And when the glow of this strange supernatural light began to struggle with the darkness of the world, then began what are known as the "dark ages." It was not that they were darker than those which had gone before; it was the beginning of a consciousness on the part of the more enlightened of the fact that they were so dark. The wall between civilization and barbarism was broken down and the darkness of the world mingled with the light that had been confined to a few, but was to shine henceforth for all men. It was the beginning of a vast struggle between intellectual night and intellectual day. And little by little the light won its way and the shadows receded, little by little the civilizing influence spread, deepening the purposes and ennobling the lives of men. Little by little the arts and sciences regained what was lost, and more also, not in the narrow theatre of the past, but all over the wide world.

And how was this accomplished? By teaching the arts and the sciences? No; by teaching the worship of God. What did the work? Was it done by great universities, supported by such endowments as the Carnegie Fund, presided over by men who gave their whole lives to the study of natural sciences and secular literatures? No. It was the monk that modern culture so despises who did the work. It was the monk, preparing men for the next world, who made men fit to live in this. It was the monk who kept in his cells the treasures of ancient literature that would have been lost otherwise, and reproduced them in the scriptorium of the monastery. It was the monk who taught the peasant the agricultural arts and impressed upon the nobles the dignity of labor by putting his own hands to the plow—hands that were consecrated to the service of God.

Our popular histories leave us with the impression that for ten centuries at least the world stood still. Before that there were some centuries of retrogression; after it, in the fifteenth century, there was a sudden leap forward. Civilization, having slept, dreaming horrid dreams, through a long black night, leaped to its feet, wide-eyed and full of life; of a sudden, the light broke on the world like a new day radiantly beautiful. It is thrilling, but it isn't true. There were scientists between the fifth century and Leonardo da Vinci; there were schools, even common primary schools, wherever there was Christianity, from the days of Constantine. The early fathers of the church were men of culture and great intellectual power. As logicians and rhetoricians they were not inferior to the best of the pagan civilization; in philosophy they do not stand out because they did not have to create philosophical systems, they merely preached the revealed truths. That was the great task of their time, and they did it well. Plato set himself to create a philosophy, and he did it well. Archimedes was a great mechanic. Augustine was a great missionary. The Renaissance was not the flash of light that we have been trained to think it. It was only a stage in the development of civilization. That development had been going on all the time. Back in the ninth century, there had been common schools under Christian control in the provinces over which Christianity was exercising its civilizing influence; they existed in Ireland, they existed in France, they existed in Germany.

The church had had its popes who were school-teachers and scientists. One of them in the tenth century had invented an abacus for the study of geometry. Another, according to the old records, was teaching astronomy and geography by means of terrestrial globes.

Oh, yes, a great many people did think the world was flat; and there was a great deal of ignorance—there is to-day. The mass of men then didn't know any more about the shape of the earth than the mass of men now know about the history of those ages. But they were learning, just as we are learning. The strictly religious monastic schools were teaching them little by little, as the human race is always taught; teaching them with the purpose of saving their souls from perdition, and with the effect of deepening and widening steadily the circle of secular knowledge.

That is the work that religion was doing for the human race—for its secular interest, I mean, not its spiritual salvation. Prejudice would teach us otherwise, but prejudice is blind.

"The one-sided and superficial literature of the 'Enlightenment,'" says Frederick William Foerster, "is raked for all possible instances of abuses, for all the degenerate and barbarous symptoms that have marked the history of the church in Europe. The eye of the searcher, like that of a nerve specialist, is on the *qui vive* for the abnormalities of human life. All these abuses and exaggerations are represented as the essential content of what was in reality a rich and magnificent development of civilization. And all this is done with such absolute lack of appreciation that the reader is forced to say to himself: Well, a man who wants to look at matters in that way, who in the long development of Christian civilization can see nothing but mental derangement and delirium, who thinks that the unapproachable masterpieces of medieval architecture, the rich harvest reaped in all arts and crafts, the incomparable spirit of sacrifice, the living, breathing literature, the deep and sincere holiday joyfulness of those times, who thinks that all this has no inner connection with the living, all-embracing, all-penetrating spiritual power of the Christian church, that it is no testimony to her civilizing creative energy —well, let him think so, if he will. Such a man will do no harm, for he stands too far away from the mainsprings of life to exercise any very deep influence whatsoever. Books written in this spirit are read— and forgotten. To drag abuses to light is an easy task anywhere in history, and especially in those periods when institutions with really sublime ideas and far-seeing plans have undertaken the task of recreating degenerated civilizations, since such institutions must look for success to the coöperation of just those human powers which they intend to elevate and educate. Imagine 'evolutionary' ethics endeavoring to civilize the disorganized and unorganized masses which the migration of nations offered to the educators of the early middle ages!"

This is from the pen of a man regarded for years in Europe as perhaps the greatest living teacher. He was for years the foremost among the champions of "ethical culture"; his father was devoted to the cause of non-religious ethical education; his own education was conducted on that line, and he grew into manhood an enthusiast for freedom of thought from "religious shackles," and the development of man's moral nature according to the rationalist formula. He has been the editor of the newspaper organ of the International Ethical Culture Society and the international secretary of that society.

Mr. Foerster, too, has an answer to the question, Can morals be taught? His answer is more to the point than is that furnished by the experience of the Spartans, for it deals with the teaching of morals in modern conditions of life. He lives to-day, he is the most modern of moderns. He knows the ethical culture theory and practice from alpha to omega; he has been through all that. This is his career, briefly sketched: His father, William Foerster, an astronomer of note and a privy councillor at one time to the

German emperor, was among those intellectual Germans who were leaders in the rationalist movement and who regarded revealed religion as of no further value to humanity. The theory of ethical culture, of supplying the moral need the abolition of religion had created, made a strong appeal to him, and on the model of the Society for Ethical Culture founded in New York in 1876 by Dr. Felix Adler, he founded an ethical culture society in Berlin. In the spirit and according to the rule of the new cult William Foerster educated his son Frederick, who was born in Berlin in 1869. No religious influence played any part in the training of the younger Foerster, who partook of his father's enthusiasm for ethical culture. Frederick was so ardent, indeed, in the cause that he resolved to make character-training his life-work. It was characteristic of him that he recognized the educational value of the study of human life itself. After obtaining his degree of doctor of philosophy from the University of Freiburg in 1893, he spent two years journeying among the poor in Germany, England, and America, studying at first hand and with his own eyes the conditions he hoped to ameliorate if not remedy by the magic of a rational cultivation of natural morality. In 1895 he became the editor of *Ethische Kultur*, the official organ of the German ethical culture movement; and so brilliant was his work, so ardent his spirit, so truly did he typify the movement at its best, that the first International Ethical Culture Congress, held in Zurich the following year, created the office of international secretary and elected Foerster its first incumbent. No finer selection could have been made. Young, strong, profound, sincere, he was an ideal champion of the cause. He was ready to give proof of the sincerity of the faith that was in him, and he did give it—an article of his on the Kaiser and the Social Democracy was condemned as treasonable, and its author offered the choice between retraction and imprisonment. He suffered the imprisonment. Since 1896 his home has been in Zurich and his principal work has been the teaching of ethics in the public schools of that city, although he is also a lecturer at the University of Zurich.

This is the character of the man, this his training and experience, who has found that ethical culture must be alive or it will not work; that the conscience of man is not a physical organ, but a part of his soul. For a little more than a year it has been realized on both sides that his path and that of the society of which he was a leader for seventeen years are divergent instead of coincident or parallel, and that the distance between them is widening rapidly.

"My one-time persuasions," he says, "were the result, not merely of my consistently irreligious education, but likewise of the bookworm enlightenment that our universities offer to the young man of to-day —an enlightenment that keeps him a stranger to real life, that allows no deep insight into the shadows of modern society. At one time I was a very earnest free-thinker, and endeavored to follow the system to its deepest conclusions. But just the earnestness of my endeavors led me to bid adieu to free thought. . . . Instinctively I felt it my duty to remodel my views by contact with real life. So I interrupted my academical studies soon after receiving the degree of doctor, devoted myself for two years to the study of the labor problem and youthful delinquents, gave myself to practical personal care of the poor, made journeys to other lands to study the same problems, and finally, in Zurich, began the practical work in the formation of character. The insight thus gained into real life, into the concrete problems of the living man, is the real cause of my inner transformation. I began to see Christianity with other eyes. Christianity, until then, had seemed to be a foreign, antiquated element of life —now I saw that I had been a stranger to life, a dead man. 'When the dead rise!' And I am fully persuaded that this same method of living observation of life and self would bring many of my contemporaries to the views which I to-day uphold. Nor could they rest satisfied with the shallow, diluted Christianity of modern academic culture, but would be drawn by the concrete knowledge of what is human—all too human—to understand anew and revere anew the superhuman grandeur of Christ."

Dr. Foerster has had the usual experience of a rationalist who uses his reason instead of setting it on a shrine and swinging a censer before it: the reason-worshipers announced sadly that he was "ultramontane," "orthodox," "Catholic." It was too bad, something like his being mentally deranged. That is the habit of rationalists; a convenient habit it is, too, because you do not have to answer one who is "ultramontane," or "orthodox," or "Catholic," any more than you would have to answer one who is mentally deranged; you just announce the fact and let it go at that. But there is a new mental atmosphere in Germany—they do have new mental atmospheres over there every once in a while—and in the case of Dr. Foerster it doesn't go at that. In the first place, Dr. Foerster isn't "ultramontane," and he isn't "Catholic," and he is regarded quite generally in German educational circles as the deepest student and most successful practitioner of character cultivation now living. Consequently the German world, or rather the Germanic world, that listened to "ethical culture" because he preached it, is eager for his new message, and rationalism is quite put out about it. To those here who hesitate to adopt a just, common-sense plan of restoring religion to its proper place in the training of the young because of an unrecognized, but for that reason all the more powerful, prejudice against the Catholic Church, the defense of his recent views by this non-Catholic German scholar should be interesting.

"Especially emphatic has been the protest," he says, "against the 'Catholic' tone of the book, and not a few have stamped the author as a 'strictly orthodox Catholic.' The whole proceeding is a proof of the narrow-mindedness with which, in the present clash of sects and parties, the majority of men open a book that does justice to their opponent, or even affirms that much may and should be learned from an opponent who enjoys the advantage of centuries of experience in the field that is in question. These years have furnished me with many instances of the incredible prejudices with which so many 'unprejudiced' scholars regard the Catholic Church. It is for them an unquestioned dogma that every position which she defends is nonsense, disease, superstition. They cannot grasp the idea of a really unprejudiced observer arriving by impartial research and earnest meditation at the conclusion that certain educational ideas of the Roman Church are the unavoidable consequences of any science of life and soul that penetrates below the surface. Such a concession on the part of a non-Catholic is simply unallowable. Truth ceases where Catholicism begins. To find truth beyond that line is to forfeit one's title in the aristocracy of science. That is the 'prescribed route' of modern radicalism, and woe to the man who leaves the beaten path! What does it matter that scientific earnestness and honest conviction force him to do so? He is stigmatized with the fatal epithet of 'ultramontane' and thus made harmless. I ask my honorable opponents to keep one fact clearly before their eyes: the truth and indispensability of an idea or method for culture and civilization do not become null and non-existent just because that idea is upheld by the Roman Catholic Church. Or is it so absolutely impossible to conceive that this church, during the centuries which she has been engaged in caring for souls, has discovered one and the other essential truth of pedagogy and civilization, truths that must be admitted even from a non-Catholic standpoint as soon as the searcher digs into the psychological and ethical depths of the problem in question?"

Two facts stand out, then. First, the human mind of all ages agrees that the purpose of education must be moral. Second, the highest authority on ethical culture declares that ethical culture is insufficient.

"I know very well," he says, "how far 'purely human' inspiration will lead the world of youth. . . . I understand what a severe blow it must be to those who would replace religion by ethics when my convictions force me to oppose them with all my energy, when I assert that just my thorough-going efforts in purely ethical instruction have convinced me that such instruction is insufficient—yea, that the ethical appeal, in order to become deeper, is forced by its own inner psychology to become religious; that the natural disposition to good must be impregnated, clarified, fortified by superhuman ideals before it can cope successfully with the inborn tendencies to evil."

On the 13th day of July, 1787, the Confederate Congress, consisting of the delegates of the United States of America appointed by each State under the Articles of Confederation, passed what was known as the Northwest Ordinance for the government of the territory of the United States northwest of the River Ohio. By the authority vested in them, and for the purpose, as they expressed it, of "extending the fundamental principles of civil and religious liberty which formed the basis whereon these republics, their laws and constitutions, are erected," they did ordain, as follows:

"Religion, morality and knowledge being necessary to good government and the happiness of mankind, schools and the means of education shall be encouraged." (Art. 3.)

These delegates were those to whom we appropriately refer as the Fathers of the Nation. They were making the fundamental law for a new territory. They were expressing fundamental ideas. It is plain that they regarded "schools and the means of education" as places and instruments for the instruction of the young in "religion, morality and knowledge." Moreover, they gave enduring recognition to their belief that not only did education, properly considered, include instruction in religion, morality and knowledge, but that these three purposes or ends of instruction were "necessary to good government," and, being necessary to good government, should be recognized, provided for and encouraged as essentials of government, if it were to be good government.

There could be no clearer proof than this that the conception of education and morality as combined and interdependent factors was fundamental in this government and informed our constitution. With the help of this illuminating statute we may with certainty define the precise meaning of those subsequent constitutional provisions of the Federal Government and the various States which have been wrenched from their original purpose. They were a simple prohibition framed in the interests of justice, and intended to preclude the possibility of the use of public funds for proselyting purposes by any one church. Not religion, but discrimination against religion, was what the Fathers of the Republic feared.

CHAPTER X

WHERE THEY BLEW THE LIGHT OUT

THE destruction of religion in a nation must carry with it what has been in all times and among all nations a part of religion. Morality has been always the content of religion; and this is not surprising, because morality is truth and religion is truth, and truth is true in all directions. So you cannot say to a man: "It is true that virtue is a real thing, but it is not true that God is a real thing." "If there is no God," the man will say back to you, "then what is virtue?" And you will be put to it for an answer. Never in the history of the world has there been a definition of virtue comprehensible by any considerable number of human beings which was not predicated upon the existence of a God. Never in the world has there been a law behind which was not a force. Never in physics or logic has there been an effect without a precedent cause.

It is a law of motion that the initial impetus will always hold in a moving body; matter in progression may be deflected from its course by the intervention of other forces, but the impulse imparted at the beginning will incline eternally toward the original direction. The initial impulse of Socialism was materialistic. It was projected in that line. Efforts have been made by politicians here and elsewhere, but particularly here, to change its direction, but these efforts have always been futile because the impulse was stronger than the politicians. Christian ministers have tried to draw Socialism into coincidence with Christianity, but the result has been invariably that they have been drawn away from Christianity. Their little disclaimers have been drowned in the great materialistic chorus of the movement. The economic philosophy builded upon "the materialistic conception of history" cannot be wrenched from that foundation. You may find here and there a Socialist who protests that Socialism does not clash with the family ideal, but you will have to seek him among thousands of writers and speakers who frankly denounce marriage as a bourgeois arrangement altogether incompatible with economic freedom and quite incapable of surviving capitalism. The Socialist who tries to reconcile his economic creed and his religion will be found to have so modified his religious beliefs in the process of assimilation as to make such a reconciliation possible only at the expense of his religion. It is never his Socialism that is strained; it is always his belief in a personal Creator and Ruler of the universe. Among the most paraded of the so-called Christian Socialists is the Rev. George D. Lunn, mayor of the city of Schenectady. Dr. Lunn has vigorously asserted many times that they are unfair who assert that Socialism undermines religion. He made such a declaration in a debate at Hartford, Connecticut, when I was his opponent; but with questions and quotations I was able to force from him the admission that if compelled to choose between religion and Socialism, he would choose Socialism. What kind is the Christianity of a Christian minister who admits his willingness to relinquish what must be infinite and eternal truth in order that he may retain what he himself describes as a mere economic programme? If Christian be an adjective of any meaning at all, then Dr. Lunn is not a Christian Socialist, for no man, knowing what Christianity is, and what Socialism is, can be both. It does not answer the argument to say that there are many kinds of Christians. There is no kind of Christian who is an atheist. There can be no kind of Christian who believes in the "materialistic conception of history." Catholic and Protestant may differ as to the meaning of some things Christ said, but between them there can be no difference of opinion as to what he meant when he said he was the Son of God. Catholic and Protestant believe what Christ said—that is what makes both of them Christians—but no man who does not believe what Christ said has any right to be called a Christian. Having ceased to believe, he has ceased to be a Christian; he has become a mere Socialist bell-wether.

Virtue can be understood only in terms of religion. Granted that there is a God, and the conception of certain things in violation of his law being evil and certain other things in harmony with his law being virtuous becomes a necessary consequence. But you cannot destroy a belief in God and retain your conception of morality any more than you can hang your hat on a hook if there be no hook.

It is often pointed out that some atheists live virtuous lives. But that is sorry evidence. Men are not all alike temperamentally. Some have an inclination toward one vice, some toward another; some find pleasure in the mere fact that there is less danger in abstinence than in indulgence. But when temptation comes to the atheist, he has no rational ground for resistance. If it be in the form of a fair face, how easily can he convince himself that matrimony, or whatever obstacle may intervene, is but a mere conventional superstition—a convention to bend before which is unworthy a bold modern spirit living in an age that has outgrown its intellectual swaddling-clothes!

The believer in God may sin—and human nature, being weak, does sin—but he knows he sins, and knows that his religion has no sympathy for such euphemisms as "soul-mates" and "affinities." The law of God is the law of God—to obey it may be hard, but to obey it is not impossible.

The destruction of religion in a nation must carry with it, then, all the fruits of religion. You can't grow apples without a tree. But a vast attempt to destroy religion may have a secondary consequence: it may produce reaction. I think this is just what we are beholding in the French nation. It was in France that infidelity became a philosophy first. It was Voltairism and Encyclopedism that found political expression in the French Revolution. It went the mad length of its tether, through blood and bombast, to the length of exalting a poor painted girl of the streets and worshiping her. Poor tinselled hysteric—they called her the Goddess of Reason, but the world will laugh at her for generations as the Goddess of Rationalism!

Then came the reaction—Robespierre's Supreme

Being festival, then constitutionalism, then absolutism—extreme to extreme! So run things in France.

Socialism has had a try in Paris. Men still living remember the Commune. True, it wasn't a fair trial; even if it had been a decent system, it couldn't have done much under the circumstances. So the Commune didn't do much or go far—the murder of some nuns and priests was its most notable accomplishment before MacMahon's guns blasted it out.

But of later years Socialism has had a fairer chance. It did get a foothold among the people, particularly in the cities. It elected deputies from the departments—numerously, so that it gained control of the governing chamber. It made its spokesmen premiers; it seized the French schools; it confiscated the churches; it had its mad way, and passed resolutions denying the existence of God. This is what Socialism meant in France; this is what it did. There is an impression in America that the separation of church and state in France meant what the same term means to us. Protestant America accepted what was done as the expropriation of the Roman Catholic Church from public benefices. Protestant writers who were on the scene have striven in vain to show how false is this idea. Protestant ministers in France know better what Socialism has done than do those of America, and from Protestant no less than Catholic sources in France has come the indignant protest against what there appears in its true light—that of an attack, not on Catholicity alone, but upon belief in God.

Mr. Vance Thompson, Protestant journalist, long resident in Paris, long-time lover and student and interpreter of France, wrote these words for *Everybody's Magazine* in 1907:

" . . . By a vote of nearly three to one the representatives of the French nation turned out the light in heaven. It was a prodigious event. Two thousand years a star stood over Bethlehem. 'We have put out that star forever!' cried the orator. He was Viviani, a desperate lawyer, politician, journalist, a Socialist who had fought his way to power with the ruthless courage of a medieval bravo. Having been personally informed of the non-existence of God, he announced the fact simply and frankly: 'Aye, there was a deceptive light in heaven, but we have put it out forever!' By 'we' he meant the brawling cohort grouped at the left of the chamber—the cohort of Socialistic Greeds. . . . By 'we' Viviani meant all the Voices and Appetites round the swill-trough of the state. . . . When the French chamber passes a new law it orders it printed on huge posters and posted up all over France —at every street corner, in every hamlet, on wayside barns and fences. I have forgotten which Juarez rose and demanded that Viviani's speech should be placarded over France; but by a vote of nearly three to one the order was made. And for weeks after— even to this day—the walls and boardings proclaimed the interesting fact that the French Assembly had decreed the non-existence of God and turned out the light that shone once upon a time overhead. . . . The only worship they have is that of the trough; immediately after banishing God from heaven (by a vote of nearly three to one) they decided (by a nearly unanimous vote) to double their own salaries. Thus, having disposed of the necessary preliminaries, the Chamber of Deputies went on about the business of passing laws for the confiscation of what property it had not yet taken from the church."

This is the evidence of one Protestant authority. It was written early in 1907; it was published in the March number of *Everybody's* of that year. Two years later a series of articles on France and the "Separation Law" appeared in the Boston *Traveller*. They were written by Mr. Alvan F. Sanborn, who is described by the *Traveller* as "a Protestant in religion, a native of Massachusetts, who has devoted all his life to the study of social problems, and whose book, *Paris and the Social Revolution*, is accepted as being the last word on the description of the social forces at work in the French capital."

Because Mr. Sanborn's articles would occupy more space than this little work can afford, I shall merely take from them paragraphs here and there. The following is the first that arrests my attention:

"A former principal of an American normal school, who had made a life study of the educational methods of his own and foreign countries, told me in 1897 or 1898 that a certain Dominican school, not a hundred leagues from Paris, was the best boys' school he had ever seen. So convinced was he of its superiority that, stern Protestant though he was, he confided his grandson to it for a couple of years. He never saw cause to regret his action. The worthy man, who is dead now, would be uneasy in his grave if he knew that this very school had been closed by an order of the state."

WHERE THEY BLEW THE LIGHT OUT

Here is the second paragraph of my selection:

"Illiteracy is increasing in France at a surprising rate in consequence of the closing of the schools of the religious orders, which the state is unable to replace, and will be unable to replace for a long while to come."

Mr. Sanborn bases this assertion upon a statistical table issued by the Minister of War. In 1905 there were 321,000 conscripts. In 1907 there were 314,000 conscripts. The decrease in the number of conscripts is two per cent. In 1905 the number of absolute illiterates recruited was 10,644. In 1907 it was 11,062. The increase is nearly four per cent. Mr. Sanborn points out that prior to 1906 the rate of illiteracy had been diminishing; that after 1906 it increased; and that it was in 1906 that the French army began to recruit from the boys who were at school when the war on religious education broke out.

I shall pass over what Mr. Sanborn has to say relative to the "laicization" of the hospital and charitable institutions, and quote him with reference to the suppression of the industrial schools:

"The World's Fair of 1900," he says, "furnished even more convincing proof of the importance of the part played by the church in providing manual and industrial training. The jury which passed judgment on the institutions for the development of the working-people [a jury of which, by the way, Jane Addams of Hull House was the American member] awarded the greater part of the prizes to Catholic institutions. The member of the jury to whom fell the labor of preparing its report said, among other things: 'The jury made just as pressing appeals to lay as to the religious societies. It did its utmost to enlist the coöperation of both the unsectarian and the sectarian enterprises, and its surprise was great to discover the zeal of the Catholics and the indifference of the laity. We have no need to seek the cause of the abstention of some and the enthusiasm of others. Our task consists solely of judging freely the exhibits which have been presented for our examination, and it is my duty, after ridding myself of every political and religious preoccupation and influence, to give the impression made upon me by the exhibits sent to the Palace of Social Economy and to the Catholic Pavilion at Vincennes. In the conflict with the sufferings of the people, it is the Catholics who have been the leaders of the vanguard. The ameliorations we owe them have been inspired by sentiments of humanity to which only a narrow sectarianism can refuse to do justice. We may hold opinions quite different from those of the promoters of all the works which are the subject of this report regarding the interpretation of the religion of charity and love whose treasure of compassion Christ spread over the world, but there is not a person of good faith who does not recognize the beneficent virtue of their institutions and the extent of their influence.

"Barely a year," Mr. Sanborn continues, "after this brilliant demonstration at the Paris Exposition of the tremendous value of the church schools in the training of industrial workers, came the attempt to suppress them by the law against the congregations. The broad-minded and ordinarily gentle president of the jury referred to above, Anatole Leroy-Beaulieu, was roused to indignation and exclaimed: 'What societies exhibited most in this class; what enterprises were the most rewarded—and God knows that the jury named by M. Millerand was in no wise tainted with clericalism? The exhibits which were the most numerous, the exhibits which obtained the first prizes or the gold medals, were mainly religious and especially Catholic exhibits. The greatest number of prizes given to institutions for the improvement of the working-people were given, willy-nilly, by a lay jury to Christian undertakings, to the very societies, to the very congregations accused of fomenting ignorance in the people; and it is to these associations, inspired by evangelical charity, that the spirit of intolerance and sectarianism pretends to refuse the liberty and even the right to exist, as if they were immoral and anti-social institutions!' "

Mr. Sanborn's fifth article opens with this paragraph:

"The withdrawal of religious instruction from the public schools, and the closing of the schools of the religious orders, have been followed by an appalling increase in crime, particularly juvenile crime. The attempt to substitute the teaching of morals for the teaching of religion is a failure."

Mr. Sanborn says the chairman of the committee on judiciary reform "recently reported"—this was in 1909—"an increase of eighty per cent. since 1901 in the total number of crimes in the country." He quotes this from Dr. Gustave Lebon, scientist and sociologist: "Criminality has augmented in proportions that are veritably terrifying: thirty per cent. for the murders, while the sum for the criminality has doubled in five years." Remember that this is in 1909 —the school-boy of 1901, when the law against the church schools was promulgated, is now from sixteen to twenty-three years of age. "The average age of criminals," says Mr. Sanborn, "is getting to be younger and younger. More than sixty per cent. of the inmates of the 'maisons centrales' are under twenty-nine years of age. Many of the bands of 'Apaches' consist of boys of from fourteen to seventeen, and their chiefs are often not more than nineteen or twenty."

Readers of newspapers will consider that matters in France have not improved much since Mr. Sanborn wrote the paragraphs just quoted. Twice or three times a week the newspapers contain despatches relative to the reign of terror from "Apaches" in the French capital. The following table is from an article on the automobile bandits of Paris, published in the New York *Sun* of April 14, 1912:

CRIMES COMMITTED BY PARIS MOTOR-CAR BANDITS.

Nov. 27, 1911.   Chatelet-en-Brie.
Chauffeur murdered and automobile stolen.
Dec. 14, 1911.   Boulogne-sur-Seine.
Automobile of M. Norman stolen.
Dec. 21, 1911.   Paris.
Attempt to murder Caby, bank messenger, in the Rue Ordener.

WHERE THEY BLEW THE LIGHT OUT

Jan. 31, 1912.   Paris.
  Bank messenger named Gouy-Paillet robbed of $30,000.

Jan. 31, 1912.   Les Aubrais, near Orléans.
  Freight station robbed; two men wounded.

Jan. 31, 1912.   Angerville.
  Revolver battle with burglars in which a policeman was killed and his murderer committed suicide.

Feb. 27, 1912.   St. Mande.
  M. Buisson's automobile stolen.

Feb. 27, 1912.   Paris.
  Policeman Garnier shot in the Rue du Havre in trying to stop auto containing bandits.

Feb. 29, 1912.   Pontoise.
  Attempt to rob the office of a notary named Tuitant.

Mar. 20, 1912.   Chaton.
  Attempt to rob automobile garage.

Mar. 25, 1912.   Montgeron.
  Chauffeur named Nathille murdered on the road by men who stole the automobile.

Mar. 25, 1912.   Chantilly.
  Société Générale's bank robbed; two clerks killed; $10,000 stolen.

As we consider the number and character of these crimes of violence, we cannot exclude from our minds a not dissimilar situation in New York. Here, too, we have had secularization of the schools. Here, too, we have developed a class of young criminals who possess nerve and cunning and utter contempt for human life and all law, human and divine. Our police arrest youths in the commission of burglary and find them students in a Brooklyn college of medicine. Bank messengers and jewellers are robbed in the very heart of the Borough of Manhattan by automobile

[213]

bandits. The streets of New York are hardly more safe in broad daylight than were the heaths of England when vizored gentlemen rode them up and down after nightfall, a century and a half ago. Is there not food for reflection in the analogy? Will those who stand for the secularized school in the name of progress stop to think and ask themselves if this be progress?

To return to France, where Socialism blew out the lights of heaven, and Mr. Sanborn, who writes from the darkened nation. "It must not be supposed," he says, "that only the Catholics were troubled by this onslaught. The French Protestants saw so clearly that the suppression of the religious orders was directed less against the Catholic religion than against the Christian idea itself, that several of their writers and scholars, among them Auguste Sabatier, dean of the Faculty of Protestant Theology at Paris, issued a protest against the passage of the law. The Protestant Wilfred Monod published a sort of catalogue of the acts of intolerance, bigotry, sacrilege, vulgarity, and violence of which the free-thinkers had been guilty, which was a more terrible indictment than any Catholic, probably, has drawn up against them. Even a Protestant pastor away off in the heart of the Cévennes was impelled to cry out: 'I am a Protestant, but I am a Christian before I am a Protestant!' Pastor Charles Wagner, well known in America as the author of *The Simple Life*, wrote to a prominent defender of the law: 'According to you, free thought is merely anti-clerical and is not anti-religious. This assertion is too violently contradicted by the facts to be maintainable except as a declaration of an ideal. The anti-religious spirit is so emphasized in the various public demonstrations of free thought at which we assist that morality itself is attacked, in the name of intellectual independence, as a symptom of clericalism. The formula, "Neither God nor master," which repudiates, as masters, conscience and the moral law itself, and the coarse rhymes that are shrieked with ostentation, permit us no illusion regarding the point at issue.' "

They have had secularization of the schools in France. We are having it here. They have had a wave of Socialism in France. We are having it here. Similar causes will have, everywhere and forever, similar effects.

But there is a new note in France; there is a sign of the inevitable reaction. Within half a year there has been a revival of the old French spirit of patriotism. The Red Socialists, seemingly in full career, have met a wave of national sentiment that grows with every hour, and is filling the Socialist politicians with confusion and dismay.

One of the last of Mr. Sanborn's articles was headed, "The French Still a Religious People." It prophesied a reaction. There are signs that it is at hand. The high tide of Socialism in France has been reached. The ebb has set in.

CHAPTER XI

SOCIALISM

THE mind that is not strong shuns mental labor. Reasoning is difficult: it is as wearisome for the intellectually weak to follow truth from premise to premise as it is for the physically weak to attain a distant goal step by step. The latter want to jump at the goal, the former at the conclusion. This is the cause of Socialism's strength and its weakness politically. The pull of truth, that is like the pull of gravitation, is upon it; as it swells in volume and gathers political strength, it verges more and more from the wild unreason of its founders and toward the sobriety and sense of the facts of life. There is hope in this, but not for Socialism. When, as a political movement in this or any other country, it has become a formidable contestant for the control of the government, it will have abandoned its international character, its materialistic philosophy, its economic vagaries. The substance of much of these it has already relinquished, although it clings tenaciously to the terms in which they were once expressed. It is interesting to follow the unfolding process, to watch each successive explication as it sheds like decaying husks the outer coverings that were for a time regarded as the movement itself, revealing with each such divestment a new vesture resembling more nearly than its predecessor the silk hat and frock-coat of ordinary humdrum political partisanship. The early Utopians had their little day and were driven out as mad dreamers by the "scientists" of the movement. History laughs at the expulsion because mad dreamers have successfully maintained coöperative commonwealths, but "scientists" never have been able to do so. The "scientists" builded their philosophy upon what they assumed to be Darwin's destruction of belief in revealed religion. Therefore the "materialistic conception of history"; therefore the hatred of religion as a device of the capitalist to oppress the proletarian; therefore the solidarity and class consciousness of the wage-earners; therefore the hatred of patriotism and its symbols and the devotion to internationalism and its symbols; therefore the reduction of all values to terms of labor power, and the reduction of all labor to terms of physical pressure. God was gone, everything was due to matter; therefore everything must be materially possessed and materially enjoyed. Over this phantasmagoria of false conclusions still gleamed the light of the Utopian dream. It attracted the oppressed and the generous-hearted but weak-minded; led them like a will-o'-the-wisp into the wilderness. From it issued the smell of death—for to the materialist life is but a process of death, and death another form of life—and this attracted the atheists. The materialist philosophy of it removed the moral check to material passions and suggested irresponsibility for their indulgence, and there flocked to it the licentious, hopeful of a society in which they could "live their life" and be unashamed of what kind of a life it was. God, patriotism, matrimony—none of these had a place in "scientific" socialism.

But the Socialistic party, when it began to deal practically with facts, became parties, and these parties are each day and hour becoming less Socialistic. Your modern Socialist teacher has abandoned "the materialistic conception of history" by gradations, the first of which was "the economic interpretation of history." Spargo's construction of Marx and Engels would hardly be recognized by these "scientists," I am afraid. The politicians of the movement say it isn't necessary to be an atheist any longer. As they interpret Marx's teachings in a fashion that would have shocked Marx, so they now assume "evolution" to mean something of which Darwin never dreamed. They are getting chary of the religious issue; they are less stressful with regard to the Spartan system of dealing with children. We are still to have matrimony, although there is still the suggestion that it is going to be an easy kind of matrimony. Class consciousness, by modern gloss, means that we are all conscious that we belong to the same class. Internationalism or political solidarity is gone; the declaration that the American Socialist party is of a piece with the world movement no longer appears in the American Socialist platform. At the last national convention the international principle went to smash on the question of Chinese immigration. The Mongolian proletariat is shut out of the world movement.

These modifications of Socialism, which the very laws of political development constrained upon it, render it less dangerous as a political movement. Every movement of a political nature must approximate the real laws of development as it approaches a real contact with such laws. A man may make the maddest speeches with respect to the methods of operating a steam-engine, and may have the most delightful theories as to the mechanical marvels possible with respect to such operation, but when he gets down to running a real steam-engine he must run it the way it was made to run, and the value of his plans will depend altogether upon their coincidence with the mechanical facts. Consequently, the economic dangers of Socialism are not as real as might be supposed. They may do some temporary damage, but they can have no permanent place in human history and in social organization. Because, however, these political dangers are not real, the moral dangers must not be considered as negligible. Everything that makes for a diffusion of the sense of obligation, that divests the individual of his accountability and seeks to spread that accountability over the whole of society, loosens the moral system and opens the way to a moral decadence which no nation has ever been able to survive. Some political leaders of Socialism to-day may teach a certain nebulous doctrine which they conceive to be Christianity, but those who join the movement are given for study the books and pamphlets of extreme radicals whose teachings, doctrinal and moral, are opposed to every tenet that even the broadest interpretation will allow to be Christian. The Christian who adopts Socialism as a political or economic plan of amelioration finds himself in close

association with pseudo-philosophers who are even
more concerned in overturning the laws of Heaven
than in subverting the laws of men. It is all very well
for the Rev. Dr. Lunn to say that the literature of
atheism can do no harm. The fact is that it can and
does do harm. The fact is that it can and does per-
vert the minds of men who are easily turned from
faith in religious tenets taught them in childhood to a
wild license and irresponsibility that weaken them
morally as individuals, and politically as citizens of a
republic.

Socialism represents in society at large a certain
confluence of aberrant thought. If we can conceive
of living thought in the form of an effluent from the
brains of millions of individual thinkers, we can visu-
alize the various currents in the living intellectual sea.
Some of those currents represent the sane thought of
mankind. Others represent the thought that swerves
from the standard of sanity and is contributed by
minds differing more or less from the normal mind of
man. There have been millions of these currents and
eddies in the intellectual history of the human race.
They have existed in every age. They have been distinguished generally by the significant terminative
"ism." Common, healthy minds have always looked
with suspicion upon an "ism." Before Marx and
Engels the "isms" were very numerous. Social paranoia divided itself into countless little intellectual
kinks. Since Marx and Engels these little individual
"isms," in accordance with the law of a psychological
principle of gravity, have been attracted toward the
greatest and latest of all the "isms" of history. For

the first time in all the world of time, insanity has been systematized, organized, and utilized as a political dynamic.

It is a characteristic of paranoia that the mind so afflicted is capable of ratiocination. It isn't in deduction that the paranoiac goes astray. It is always his premises that are inaccurately framed. Socialist literature presents a startling analogy here. It has dazzled a great many men with its logic. Its premises, however, are always found to be illusory. It is this quality that has given the new "ism" its astonishing vogue in the colleges and universities. The proportion of university thought that differs from the normal takes naturally and eagerly to Socialism. Man's limited knowledge compels him to start all his reasoning processes with an assumption of some kind. He must assume some undemonstrated, and quite possibly undemonstrable, hypothesis to be true. Nature seems to provide those who are sane with an instinct which guards them against serious error. It is the lack of this instinct that makes the "Intellectual" paranoiac. Consequently, the recently fashionable theories which were the exigents of the science of half a century ago have been unquestioningly accepted as a philosophical basis by the so-called "Intellectuals" of our universities. These theories, which took the form of monism, or a belief in the universality of matter in this universe of ours, very naturally led to the political and economic philosophical formula which has become more and more prominent within the last years as Socialism. No student of the subject can read without complete bewilderment the various and contradictory definitions of Socialism which are given to the public by the Intellectuals of the movement. According to Bax, it means the casting of religion into the limbo of outused superstitions. According to Washington Gladden, it means the strengthening of the religious spirit and the putting into practice of ideals that have hitherto existed nowhere but in religion. According to Spargo in one paragraph, it is not hostile but friendly to religion. According to Spargo in another paragraph, its friendliness will consist in taking children from their mothers and having them educated by the state, without the slightest suggestion of religion, until they reach an age when their minds are capable of understanding what theology is and what effect upon it the conclusions drawn from physical phenomena must necessarily have. According to Hillquit and Benson, it conserves the family, which capitalism has destroyed. According to Bebel, the family is a development of the capitalist system, and can no more survive capital than can poverty.

No two exponents of Socialism to-day agree as to what it means in their written works. Each of them has his own view, colored by his temperamental peculiarities, his desires, his affections, and his hatreds. Each of them takes the original formulation of Marx and Engels and bends it to suit his own inclination and purpose. It is only when each of them is studied, when each of them is analyzed, when each of them is probed to the bottom of his thought, that there is found in both of them the common attribute of all "Intellectual" Socialists, which is a materialistic conception of history and belief in the absolute determinative power of the economics of human life.

What is the basic idea of Socialistic philosophy? It is that society is an organism. The idea is that it is an organism, just as man is an organism. Man is a composite of smaller organisms. He is a collection of cells. Society is a composite of human organisms. It is a collection of men and women. That is the idea. The individual isn't responsible: it is the social organism that errs. If an individual commits a crime, it is his social environment that is at fault. Having set up this hypothesis, Socialist philosophy goes on to the question of reforming the social organism. It has lost interest in the individual.

Now let us examine this in the light of common experience and common sense. Let us get out of the mist of "economic determinism" and "materialistic interpretations," and other obscurities and ambiguities, and into the clear light of homely human every-day experience. Let us consider one huge difference between the social organism and the human organism which Socialism seems to have overlooked. In the human organism the sum thinks of its factors: in the social organism the factors think of the sum. Man thinks of himself as a psychological entity. Your brain-cells and heart-cells and stomach-cells do not think of you: you think of them. You realize that they are all parts of you. Your individual, complete consciousness and will combine them all. There is no class consciousness in your make-up, unless rheumatism be class consciousness in your legs. In you there is unity. But society! What is social consciousness?

Where is it? How does it function? Try to think this out for yourself. Is there any such thing? You may answer that society acts in the laws. It doesn't, and you know it doesn't. It is always some individual mind acting, and other minds agreeing. Who makes the laws? The legislature. A man draws a bill and his associates agree to it. Then it becomes a law. One individual, or more than one, want this or these changes made, and each change represents an individual will. Who interprets the law? An individual judge. Who passes upon the evidence? Twelve individual jurors, each with his individual brain and will. The individual human organism that thinks is always the thing that is conscious. It thinks about what it contains on one side, and what contains it on the other. A man's cells do not think about him: he thinks about them. Society doesn't think about men: men think about society. The individual is a concrete thing; society, an abstraction. An individual can do wrong, or do right; what society does is only what many individuals do. Therefore there is no responsibility in society, but there is responsibility in each human soul.

It would be impossible, within the brief confines of this chapter, to deal with each of the absurdities of Socialism. A few of them, however, may be briefly treated.

Socialism distinguishes between use values and exchange values. The fact that a thing created ministers to the satisfaction or necessity of its possessor gives it a use value. Socialism says air has a use value but no exchange value: a use value because all men need it to live, but no exchange value because there is so much of it that each man can get it for nothing. This is a favorite Socialist illustration. Air, they say, is not a commodity. A commodity must have an exchange value. It is exchange value that makes profit possible. And it is profit that is evil. We might pause here to ask if the use value is not simply a product of the Socialist term-factory. Why call it a value at all? It is not measurable, and a value, in the sense in which Socialists use the term value, must be measurable. When they use the term exchange value they mean a value measurable in the medium of exchange. A sheik of the desert has fifty camels. Two or three of them can have a use value. The rest are the measure of his wealth. A Hebrew patriarch has flocks of sheep. A few of them have a use value. The rest are the measure of his wealth. The sheik, by the surplus above the camels he can ride, and the patriarch, by the surplus above the sheep he can eat or shear, has the power to purchase other things he may desire. So was Ibrahim of the sandy plains a capitalist; so was David, the son of Jesse, a capitalist; so is every human being to-day who possesses a thing which others desire, and which he does not require to live, a capitalist.

Value is what men will pay for a thing they need or desire. Economically it is governed by the utility of the commodity in relation to its difficulty of attainment. Diamonds, which cannot be eaten, and the sight of which awakens a pleasurable sensation in not all human beings, have a value greater than food, without which no man can live. This is because food is easier to procure. A singer can command a salary of many thousands of dollars an hour, while a maker of clothes must labor for a few cents an hour. This is because the song of the singer is more intensely appreciated and less readily procurable. Is the inequality—the injustice Socialists call it—that pays a pittance for the hard toil of the mill-worker and a fortune for the few hours of the singer a thing of mere laws? No. Then how are you to cure it by laws? Is there compulsion now upon society to pay a large wage to one kind of worker and a small wage to another? No. Then how are you going to relieve a compulsion that does not exist? The impulse is in human nature. It is in the souls of individuals. It is of the very essence of the human make-up.

This question of values is one of the pet themes of the Socialist economist. Huge volumes have been devoted to proving that labor is entitled to all the value that labor creates. That is a good mouth-filling phrase which rolls fluently from the tongue of the soap-box orator and catches the interest and the sympathy of the man who toils. But to the toiler it has a meaning far different from that laboriously explained in Socialist writings. Although the soap-box Socialist does not mention it, the "Intellectual" insists that Marx and his associates did not mean that every shoemaker was entitled to the value of all the shoes he could make. "Social labor" is what Marx meant. "Social labor" is what becomes value when embodied in a useful or desirable article. And the "social labor" that enters into the shirt you bought is not the labor of the mill-hands who worked the machinery by which it was woven, nor the labor of the sweatshop worker who sewed it, nor that of the cutter who cut it, nor that of the buttonmaker; but is vastly more than all these. It reaches out to embrace the cotton-grower and his laborers, and the builder who builded the mill, and the brick-maker who made the brick, and the machinist who assembled the looms and the spinning machinery, and the mechanics who made the parts, and the railroad hands that aided in transportation, and so on infinitely in every direction, to the mother who bore all these and their mothers before them. "Social labor" is a symbol for an infinity. It is immeasurable. But this symbol equals value, they insist. Well, let it be so. How, then, by the statement, or even the proof, of this does Socialism help the toiler? The question is not one of conglomeration but of distribution. It is not to prove that an infinite number of immeasurable contributial values constitute a measured value that is important: it is the fair distribution of a measured value among the men who contributed their labor to the creation of the product. That is what will help the world. That is what humanity needs. What good does it do to prove that labor multiplied by x made a watch? The value of the watch is what men will pay for it. It may be twenty dollars or one hundred dollars. The problem is the distribution of that sum justly. x equals y will not do. It is not x with whom you are dealing; it is a certain John Jones who has a mouth of his own to fill, and a wife and children, all of whom have likewise mouths to fill. And John Jones cannot be fed on the symbols of unknown quantities. He cannot live on algebraic terms any more than you can put a five-dollar bill in the pocket of an algebraic term. John Jones must get a definite measurable fraction of the measured value of that watch. He can eat a fifth or a tenth of a loaf of bread, but he cannot eat a square root. He can live in half or one-tenth of a house, but not in $\frac{x}{y}$. Toilers, this huge humbug has nothing for you. You ask for bread, and it gives you a quadratic equation.

The pendulum of nonsense having swung to one extreme, it now goes to the other. Mr. Allan Benson writes a series of articles on Socialism for *Pearson's Magazine*. Perhaps Mr. Hillquit and Mr. Spargo would not admit that they represent Socialist teaching at all. But they do catch votes. For Mr. Benson does not deal in x's and y's. He finds it just as easy to substitute the word "dollars" for the algebraic symbols. There is an advantage in this, for the man in the street knows what a dollar is. And there is no disadvantage, for as long as Mr. Benson is dealing with the word "dollars," and not with real dollars, it is just as easy to perform interesting feats of legerdemain. So Mr. Benson, instead of talking of "social labor," announces cheerfully that under the coöperative commonwealth every worker is to get the equivalent of $5000 a year. That has a pleasant sound. Every man who earns less than $5000 a year will surely vote for that. There are ninety million people in the United States. I have not the census reports at hand, but shall make a liberal allowance for children (who are to be cared for by the state, and are probably to get less than $5000 a year) and reduce the number of

$5000-a-year individuals to 45,000,000. At $5000 a year the American payroll would total $225,000,000,-000. Only two hundred and twenty-five billions of dollars. Such is the "stuff that dreams are made of." Such is the stuff, also, that Socialist votes are made of.

Common ownership of productive machinery seems to be a solid in the fluidity of Socialism. It looks like something you can get hold of. Let us see. Handle it gently, for it isn't very far from the fluid state. What does it mean? What is "productive machinery"? We have the word of some modern American Socialists—Mr. Spargo, Mr. Hillquit, and Dr. Lunn among them—that it is not a spade, or a saw, or a hammer, or a seamstress's domestic sewing-machine. It is machinery such as is used in manufacture by the manufacturing corporations. We are not going to take his saw from the carpenter, nor his hammer from the blacksmith. We are going into the Steel-trust mill to take its huge equipment, and with that equipment we are going to produce railroad tracks, and the framework of buildings, and the countless other things which the Steel Trust now produces. There is to be no change in production; there will be the puddling and the rolling and the moulding, and all the processes to which steel is subjected. But in the distribution it will be different. We are producing for use now, not for profit. We shall so set our prices that each man employed in our huge plant will get a salary of $5000 a year. Puddler, roller, water-boy, engine-tender, oiler, stoker, foreman, superintendent, salesman, office messenger, bookkeeper—all of these are to get out of the value they create the equivalent of $5000 per annum. There are two hundred thousand of them. It means $1,000,000,000 a year for our product. It is like giving the stuff away. But wait. We forgot something. We have taken over the railroad, and there are some thousands employed there who must get the $5000 a year which Mr. Benson has fixed as the living wage. Of course we shall have to pay for that. Then there are the plant betterments with our five-thousand-dollar-a-year craftsmen and unskilled laborers, and we have to get their money out of our income on the products; and the five-thousand-a-year miner, and the five-thousand-a-year helpers— all these must be figured in. It will add something to the cost of steel. Then we must all have five-thousand-a-year wives and five-thousand-a-year servants, for everybody is in on this. It will add something, I'm afraid, to the price of steel. The whole thing is to be democratically managed. We are going to determine every question by vote. Here is one now; let us determine it. Boris Humphniak says puddling is a hot, hard job, and he doesn't see why he should blister and sweat while Reginald Carnegie just sits in a cool office talking to a stenographer. Comrade Carnegie explains to Comrade Humphniak that the Carnegie labor is necessary directive labor, and can be performed in the office, while the Humphniak labor is manual labor and must be performed in the puddling-room. Comrade Humphniak cannot see it. He says each man ought to take his turn at puddling and at superintending. Let us vote on it. There are a thousand puddlers, one superintendent. The vote is a thousand to one for the Humphniak proposition.

SOCIALISM

Comrade Carnegie goes down to the puddling-room, tries to puddle (to the intense joy of the other puddlers, who cease labor in order to enjoy his weak and inefficient attempts at puddling), and, blinded and exhausted, overturns a vat of molten metal; whereat those who survive are sorry, and those who do not—among whom is Comrade Carnegie—do not care any more. Meanwhile Comrade Humphniak goes into the office, lights a cigar, and neglects to give some orders; as a result of which forgetfulness on his part the mill burns down. So labor gets what labor creates. "The Revolution" is accomplished: there is no profit.

CHAPTER XII

THE NATION UNDER GOD

IN the very opening words of that address whose sentences, few in number but tremendous in power, gleam in letters of light from a dark and troubled page of our history, Abraham Lincoln said that our fathers had brought forth on this continent a nation "conceived in liberty and dedicated to the proposition that all men are created equal."

There had come a great test, he said, a mighty ordeal to try out the question whether that nation, or any other nation so conceived and dedicated, could endure. His closing words were an exhortation to the American people to resolve that the huge sacrifice of patriot life should not be made a vain and fruitless sacrifice, "that this nation, under God, shall have a new birth of freedom, and that government of the people, by the people, for the people, shall not perish from the earth."

"Under God!" When a great man greatly expresses a great truth, he sets a stumbling-block in the path of every falsehood that ever was or ever will be. When that clear, simple, sublime mind contemplated what was, what had been, and what was to be—a nation sundered by a great bleeding wound, a nation animated from its birth by the spirit of freedom and no more capable of growth and power with any other spirit than would one man be with the soul of another, a nation which was painfully but completely to cut out the cancerous growth that threatened its life—he uttered the protest I have quoted against the lie that in a free nation any man can be the chattel of another.

The moral evils that were in front of him, that he could see and touch, were human slavery and fratricidal war. But the truth he erected as a shield for the nation against them is to serve also as a shield for the nation against another and a deadlier peril that has come in another generation.

What was this conception of liberty and this dedication to the proposition that all men are created equal? It was a new thing in the world. There had been other governments conceived in liberty, but in all the history of the world there had been no government dedicated to the proposition that all men are created equal.

The Greek and Roman democracies are, when they are closely examined, very narrow indeed. Under the society which exercised the power of government was a great menial class, a servile foundation upon which society was builded. There were artisans and tradesmen who were free, but labor as such was shackled, a huge bondsman that builded and delved, and that had no rights—that was, in the dominant opinion of the day, on the level of the brutes.

And this servile class, this great mass of human labor, was greater than all the rest in bulk—among the Greeks the slave class at one time constituted nine-tenths of the population.

For centuries, however, even the approach to democracy that the Greeks and Romans knew had been

but a memory. The world lived according to the opposing political principle. The thought that lay back
of social organization was that men had been created
unequal, that some were born to govern and some to
slave; the former were the select few, the latter the
great mass. The aristocracy was entitled by right to
the profit of the fields, to preference before the courts
and in the halls of government; the mass was just a
beast of burden, base, ignoble, unworthy of consideration by the superior men.

Among all the peoples of the world the principle of
government was the principle of privilege. There had
been something to temper all this—the humanity of
those in power, and, more important than all else, the
influences of the Church of Christ; for the justice of
God, unlike the justice of man, held all men created
equal.

It was a divine ideal, then, that our fathers put into
the new nation. It was to a divine purpose that they
dedicated this republic. Men were to be free and
equal. Not equal in material things, but in moral
things. The vote of every man was to be equal to
that of every other man in the governing of the state.
The cause of every man was to be as sacred in the
courts of the land as that of every other man.

Not equal in physical strength, nor yet in intellectual strength, nor yet in circumstances of material
wealth, but as a moral being, as an entity before the
law of the land as before the justice of heaven, as a
unit in government, each man was born with the right
of equality. For this was a nation "under God," as
Lincoln said.

THE NATION UNDER GOD

There was another conception in liberty, another dedication to equality, which, however, was not "under God." It was under rationalism, under the philosophy that takes human reason out of a man's noddle and sets it on his altar, that ceases to use it because worshiping it, that deifies it, substituting it for the living God.

There were two revolutions. Almost as if it were designed as a lesson to humanity, they are set side by side. So close are they in time that some of the principal actors in the one great drama are principal actors in the other.

They are set down in history's page like two sums in mathematics side by side, so that we can see the factors and contrast the products. It is as if God said to us, "Here is the demonstration. See how, these factors chosen, this is the result, and these other factors chosen, that is the result."

What is the most significant thing we see as we look at those two portentous examples in political arithmetic? Why, this—America has no Voltaire! There is no sneering, brilliant, God-denying mind to dominate completely the mind of the nation. America has no Encyclopedists, no Intellectuals to interpose their cheap hand-made philosophy between a suffering people crushed down and brutalized by cruel privilege and the light of heaven; to substitute their joke-books and epigrams for the commandments of God.

If France before the Revolution was "a despotism tempered by epigrams," during the Revolution it was a mobocracy distempered by epigrams.

Here, then, is a difference between the moving factors. In France there was infidelity; in America there was a belief in God. France was a nation under Voltairism; America was a nation "under God."

See how these two factors worked as the problem became involved. In America a Congress assembled, as in France a parliament of the Three Estates. In America this Congress, sane, sober, stern, governs the nation in revolt until the work is done, and the marvellous new government dedicated to the proposition that all men are created equal is a vital fact in the world.

In that Congress statesmen and patriots are developed, men of the common people who can devise an instrument of government that has stood the test of time. Not superior men, not sneerers at faith in God, not Intellectuals, but men out of the ranks, wise, practical and inspired makers of a nation, whose every official declaration is a profession of faith in the wisdom and justice of the Most High.

But in that French parliament is such a gathering of self-seeking demagogues as never before the world has seen; cheap, rabid, hating and hate-inspiring politicians, rats that struggle and gnaw and squeal in the recesses of that rotting body which they are tearing down. Wit against wit, vanity against vanity, ambition against ambition, selfishness against selfishness, it was a government gone completely mad, shifting and veering at each noisy gust from the lungs of a bar-room statesman inspired of a sudden with a plan for making all men happy. Under rationalism, Liberty has gone insane.

These two huge dramas have each its principal human character, its man of whom all the world thinks when the world thinks of the drama. The nation under God had Washington, patriot and statesman, whose name was a glory even among his enemies. The nation under rationalism had Napoleon, conqueror and despot, bloodied to his boot-tops, filling Europe with fire and slaughter until his red and dripping star sank forever behind the lurid cannon smoke of Waterloo.

And now let us consider the products, the two answers worked out by these two examples in political arithmetic. The nation under philosophy ended its huge struggle in a despotism not even tempered by epigrams. Drained of its best blood, weakened in heart and in limbs, foreign kings riding at the head of their squadrons into its capital at will, the mass crushed down again and privilege enthroned again, nothing left of that great hope that raised it in revolution except the insanity, the Voltairism which is still at work.

But the nation "under God" has kept democracy alive, has advanced all the time, standing up against that bloody back-wash of the French Revolution that rocked every other government; attracting to itself the oppressed of all the world, destroying human slavery when that evil, grown strong, conflicted with the very purpose of its being; crushing out bigotry so that now Protestant and Catholic and Jew sit down at the same board to do honor to their brother American who has been elevated to the cardinalate of his church. This is the fruit of a conception in liberty and a dedication to equality of a nation "under God."

TWO AND TWO MAKE FOUR

These two things are side by side, as I have said,
and yet there is a philosophy that cannot read the lesson as it is written. Little by little that philosophy
has made headway in this country. It is not indig-
enous. The Irish potato is an American vegetable,
you know, but rationalism is not. It is something that
has been transplanted from the old world, where it
grows rank in the shadow of privilege. Free men are
rarely "free thinkers." You will always find tyranny
and Voltairism close together. And this modern rationalism is nothing but warmed-over Voltairism, although its political manifestation is not in precisely
the same form. Analysis was the social cure-all of the
Voltaire period. They were going to make all men
happy by taking things apart.

And, truly, they went the full logical length of the
formula. Not satisfied with the stage at which Intellectualism would pause—the taking apart of aristocracy—the mob took the aristocrats apart also; and
having taken monarchy apart, they must also take a
monarch apart.

And what then? Why, then the discovery by the
hungry millions that "Victorious Analysis," as Carlyle
puts it, "bakes no bread."

This formula having been found of no fruit, therefore, rationalism sets up another, a new make-believe
for victims of social injustice, which it calls Socialism.
It came out of the sick thought of atheists who looked
into themselves and thought they saw a universe. Its
fundamental assertion is that there is no God.

This is what is meant by the "materialistic conception of history," this is what they mean by their "eco-

nomic determinism." "God is a reflex of economic conditions," they say; that is, a ruling class invented him and preached him to keep a servile class in subjection.

A child may laugh at the absurdity of such a statement. Think of it! Back in the dim past, when, they would make us believe, men were just beginning to be men and leaving off being monkeys, some particularly wise anthropoid ape, some J. P. Morgan among the "missing links," conceived this vast deception in order that he might get the milk in the cocoanut, and his tailed, or rather recently detailed, brethren might be satisfied with the husks!

The men who say their illuminated reason cannot accept the idea of a God ask us to believe that; and ask us to believe that the thing was kept up through all the intervening ages, and that it is a huge, hoary imposture. Why, if it were an imposture, it was one so vast, so tremendous, so obviously beyond human cunning, that none but a God could create or sustain it.

With as broad a lie as that for a foundation, they had room to build anything. And they have builded a weird thing: Karl Marx has evolved from his inner consciousness some shadow of a shadow which he calls a labor-hour. What is it? Perhaps—although I doubt it—Marx knew, but Marx is dead.

We only know that it is not an hour of continuous labor by a skilled mechanic—any skilled mechanic; for labor, as he uses the term, means unskilled labor. That leaves us at sea again, for unskilled labor is but an arbitrary term to differentiate between those who

[239]

are in what we call the handicrafts and those who are not; in philosophy there is no such thing as unskilled labor. If I were called on to-night to go dig in a ditch, I should have to learn how to use a spade. The monkey and the millionaire are alike in this—neither of them knows how to use a spade. What, then, is an hour of unskilled labor? However, why worry about it? Our foundation, you know, is that there is no God. Whatever it is, it is to be the measure of value in the Socialist world.

All men have it; that is, all men who are not weak, or old, or too young. But never mind them; never mind anything that is sensible and true. How can a fact stand on the foundation that there is no God? If you are going to introduce facts here, they will sink right through our broad but unsubstantial base, because, while many men have seen a fog upon a mountain, no man but a Socialist has ever seen a mountain upon a fog.

Let us, then, take at its face value this labor-hour. It is to be the currency of the coöperative commonwealth that is to follow the revolution. Money is to be abolished because money is capital, and capital is a vicious oppression-serving reflex of economic conditions, devised long ago, doubtless, by that same monkey-man who invented God. It is just like religion, marriage, and patriotism, and that contemptible bourgeois weakness—morality.

They are all at war with the philosophy of Socialism, there will be no room for any of them in the co-operative commonwealth. Probably frost and snow, and birth and death also, are economic reflexes; one of these at least the rationalistic science of eugenics proposes to abolish in part; doubtless in the glad new time they will all be abolished, somehow. For that is the way all these reforms are to be accomplished—just somehow.

I have been for twenty years reading Socialist literature and attending Socialist meetings and talking to Socialist orators, in the hope that there might be something for humanity in all this, some pot of gold at the rainbow's end, and always the answer to my "How?" has been the same—first, let us have revolution, and the reconstruction will be managed somehow. The old Voltairism, the old analysis, the taking of things apart! Under God men build up, they construct; under rationalism they tear down, they destroy.

I have said this thing is of foreign origin and foreign growth. How comes it, then, that we find it here, in a nation "under God"? Because similar causes will, everywhere and forever, produce similar effects. We thrust out privilege in our Revolution, and set the face of the new nation forever against it. But it found its way in again until its recognition by the people in the form of slave-ownership led to its expulsion once more.

And now it is manifesting itself in industry, and we have labor ground down and oppressed, we have babies working in mills, we have vast populations that do not speak our language, do not understand our laws, do not live our life, but do out of their deep misery send up class hatred, flames that privilege has enkindled and that Socialism fans. In this nation, dedicated to equality, there is not equality before the law.

Some men, who fear Socialism not because it is a bad thing, but because it may hurt them, will say that this is preaching class hatred. It isn't—it is telling the truth. You cannot kill this thing with a lie. You must kill it with the truth. And when we tell this truth, when we say that in this country men are not always equal before the law, we must also say that if the courts are sometimes respecters of persons here, they are here less respecters of persons than any-where else in the world of God—for that also is true. Nowhere in the wide world has the man, naked of all rank and power and wealth, more chance of obtaining pure justice than under this flag, which Socialism would tear down and replace with its red international banner—and that is also true.

In this nation under God, of all nations, the funda-mental law prescribes absolute equality; and where there is aberration from that principle, the fault is not with the nation or its fundamental law, but with the weakness of human nature, to cure which does not lie in Socialism, but in the religion of God.

But it is true that privilege has done some evil in the courts—as, indeed, where has it not done evil? And it has done much evil in our political life. And worse still, because here it cannot claim the right to rob as an open and a legal right, it has had to accom-plish its ends by stealth, by falsehood, and by bribery; and so it has weakened our morality and so affected many of us that we cannot longer bear the thought of a just and righteous God. Some divinity we must have, because privilege—wiser in its generation than Intellectualism—knows that the bare lie of a no-God will not go down with the world; but let it be a vague and far-away divinity. Let us subsidize agnosticism in the colleges by endowments made up of bonds of that corporation that has imported its thousands upon thousands of laborers whose ignorance of our language and our laws makes possible their employment for seven days a week with twenty-four-hour shifts to vary the monotony. Let us forget that "wops" are human beings made in the image of God, just as the nobility of France forgot that its "canaille" were human beings whom also God had made in his image.

Do you suppose privilege, that so forgets, wants to believe in a Christ? No—it isn't possible, comfortable. Real obligations with sharp edges are too inconvenient; a real God is too terrible. Better accept the Darwinian theory of evolution from science, now that science is getting rid of it, having found it not only unproven but unprovable; better level down all creeds so that they are all alike, which will be when they are all whittled away; better dabble in this Intellectualism of Europe, where privilege is ancient and legal and fashionable, if not respectable.

And so we create a great fund for such colleges as shall abandon Christ, having been founded in his name. We say to college presidents and college professors, "You shall have a pension in your old age, provided you have not taught as truth that Jehovah of the Jews was God, and Christ, who walked on earth, was his divine Son."

And our public schools! The pity of it! We could leave the colleges to materialism, to nothingism, if it had to be so, but are we going to sit silent by while the little children of whom Christ said, "Suffer them to come unto me," are turned over to the Intellectuals, to the teachers of cast-off science, to the materialism and nothingism whose political manifestation is Socialism?

Not if we are men with sanity left in our heads! Not if we are still a nation "under God," "conceived in liberty, and dedicated to the proposition that all men are created equal."

To pass the plastic years in a godless school, to leave it with no faith to enlighten them, with no belief in their accountability to God to hold them true, with a false notion of life and its meaning; to find the struggle for subsistence hard, and on the corner or in the club the Socialist with his gospel of hatred which he calls "class-consciousness," his sneer at God, his easy plan of conduct, and his somehow political programme of making life easy to live—what results?

What have we to oppose to all this? The truth, the American ideal of a "nation under God," conceived in liberty and dedicated to equality, which is always new because always true.

We must regain for God the children of the nation. If we were all of one creed, it might be done through our present public-school system. But we are of many creeds, so that the only practicable plan, and the only just plan, is to let each creed teach its own, and let the state pay, out of the taxes collected from all, a just compensation to such educational agency, secular or religious, for the educational work it shall perform.

In this way will we best meet this new peril; in this way will we best destroy, on the one hand, the privilege that generates class hatred, and, on the other, the false philosophy that would transmute that hatred into Socialism.

It is an evil thing we have to conquer. If it were only the Intellectuals, we might let them babble away in their own little insane asylums, while the rest of us go on with the work of the world. But here is this vast army suffering from real social injustice, and here are those Intellectuals telling this army to overturn the government, break up and throw away the Constitution, close the churches, abandon their families, and they shall have bread without sweating for it.

It is the cruellest lie that ever came out of hell. But how is the sufferer to know it is a lie? He must toil to keep breath in his body; what time has he to measure and to weigh? He knows, because the weight of it bends down his back, that life is hard, and the Intellectuals tell him they have a plan to give him life and ease and food and luxuries. "The whole wealth of the world is yours, and yet you toil and starve," they say to him. "Strike, and be—rich!" Not free, but rich.

Think of the effect of this on a man who is toiling, and who has not too much food. How can one know that their system is a dream of madmen—up there in the region above him, the Intellectuals, the smart men, the college professors, say it will be all right, and they must know.

Even high privilege says, with a propitiating smile, that "Socialism has no terrors for him"; and quite true it is too, because if privilege doesn't believe in a hereafter for its spiritual self, what need it care for the hereafter of the Republic?

Some few years ago our American Socialism spoke softly of a peaceful revolution and a ballot-box campaign and conquest. But as it grows stronger it grows bolder, and now we hear less of the peaceful revolution.

They are feeling their strength, they grow bold. The talk now is of "direct action." That means that the brute is getting thirsty for blood. That is the essential barbarism growling out a little impatiently in this philosophy that boasts that it is the next step in civilization.

In Los Angeles they take as a candidate a lawyer who has been counsel for dynamiters, just because of the significant association. Their labor organization is the Industrial Workers of the World, their cry is for the general strike.

Listen to their editor who has hurried from New York into Massachusetts, as he cries out to the poor mill-hands, who think he is leading them for their sakes, "No arbitration, no compromise!"

They do not want better wages for labor, they do not want peace—they want wide-spread industrial war, dynamiting and bloodshed, and a crashing fall of this Republic Lincoln loved, so that in their beloved revolution they may strut and gabble, cheap little warmed-over Robespierres and second-hand Mirabeaus, and try to set up their crazy government on the wreckage of a nation under God, conceived in liberty and dedicated to equality.

Blind to anything like a fact, they cannot see that this isn't France of one hundred and fifty years ago. There isn't here the depth of misery that was there, although there is more than there should be and more than there shall be. This union isn't founded on privilege, as was the tyranny of old France.

And, more than all, the faith in God still holds in America, and it is strongest and purest right on the battle-line—in the very ranks of labor from which this Socialism hopes to draw its strength. Democracy lives here still, and her strength is undiminished.

And justice—when we have made America see what justice is—will allow Religion to resume her inspiring function in the education of the child. Labor shall not drink this cup that Socialism holds to its lips and find the dregs bitter with blasted hope.

But in our coming ordeal—and he is blind who cannot see it coming—sanity and sobriety and the spirit of justice must rule our councils, as they did in that other great ordeal half a century ago.

The people's leaders must be, not demagogues, not babblers, not new-idea-every-minute reformers, not gusty mock-Mirabeaus, but men of courage and conscience and sanity and sympathy and truth. Marx must not become, but Lincoln continue to be, our ideal statesman. Not rationalism, but God, must be our guide.

And as the hope of Lincoln will come true, the dead of Gettysburg and every other field where patriots fell under the flag for which Socialism would substi-

tute its banner of blood, shall not have died in vain—
"government of the people, by the people, for the
people, shall not perish from the earth," but shall live,
blessing more and more with the fruit of justice a nation under God.